THE TENNIS DOCTOR

The Loomis family—Jim, David, Matthew, and Peggy

THE TENNIS DOCTOR

*Everything You Always Wanted to Know
about Tennis but Didn't Know Whom to Ask*

JAMES C. LOOMIS

Vantage Press
*New York/Washington/Atlanta
Los Angeles/Chicago*

FIRST EDITION

Copyright © 1983 by James C. Loomis

Published by Vantage Press, Inc.
516 West 34th Street, New York, New York 10001

Manufactured in the United States of America
ISBN: 533-05582-2

Library of Congress Catalog Card No.:82-90673

To my family and especially to my parents

Contents

Acknowledgments

TENNIS HAS BEEN a significant part of my life for twenty-five years. Former tennis standout at Dennison University, Butch Berwanger, must be given credit for my early development and enthusiasm for the sport. Without a sound foundation in anything one does, it is hard to work your way up. This is what Butch provided for me.

I would like to thank the following publishing companies for allowing me to use a quotes from their books: Harper & Row, Anna Publishing Inc., Workman Publishing Co. Inc., Little, Brown, and Co.

I would like to extend a thank-you to Bill Calloway for his help and approval on the section on plyometrics. Thank-you, Ernie Danek, for doing such a fine job on the photographs. An equally warm thank-you goes to Curt Gandy for supplying me with the well-designed illustrations.

Photographs play such an important role in any book, especially a "how-to-do" book. They give the book a sense of meaning and fullness. These photographs wouldn't have been possible without the willingness and cooperation of the many people Ernie photographed.

Scott Dorrance of French Photography, Inc. deserves credit for the fine photograph used on the cover of the book.

In addition to a photographer and players to photograph, you need a place in which to take the photographs. Special thanks to the management of the Downtown Nautilus Center, the Central Branch of the YMCA, Herb Lipsman and the Cedar Rapids Racquet Club, Dr. Huey, and St. Lukes Methodist Hospital of Cedar Rapids for their fine cooperation and use of their excellent facilities.

A special thank-you to Viva Rowray for typing my manuscript and adding to the phrasing of it.

I would like to thank Vantage Press for their faith and confidence in me and my writing ability to publish and promote this book when others would not.

Finally, a very special thank-you to my parents and family for their support and encouragement. Without them this book would not have been written.

Introduction

TENNIS IS MORE THAN merely a game. It's a total learning experience. Besides learning the sport of tennis, you also learn a lot about yourself as an individual and what makes you the way you are. The reasons why one participates are numerous: to get good exercise, to improve your skills, to test yourself, to socialize, to be part of a team, to relieve tension. And the best reason of all—to have fun! You may even have your own personal reason. But if you are not having fun on the court, it would be advisable to take up another sport. However, it's hard to have fun if you don't like the way you play. People are funny that way.

In addition to being an individual activity, tennis can also be family oriented. It's a great way to get the family together to participate physically toward a common objective—which is to have fun. I feel many families today are not as "close" or "unified" as they should be. I know one reason for this is the shape of our economy. However, we should not let that be an excuse. We need to become closer as a family and one way to do this is by participating together in a common activity such as tennis, although any other activity could work as well. Families grow up much too fast and before we know it everyone has gone their separate ways. So treasure the time you have together and use it wisely. This is the first and the last sermon you will get in this book. Maybe I got a little carried away.

The title *The Tennis Doctor* may be a little misleading since in no way, shape, or form, am I, or will I in the future become, a doctor. This book has been so named for my chapters dealing with training and conditioning, injuries involved in tennis, jogging, and how to correct the problems in your game. I have included numerous pictures and diagrams depicting all facets of the game. Besides showing you the correct stroking techniques I feel it is equally important to show some incorrect means of hitting the ball. This might enable you to pick out a flaw in one of your strokes. You must be able to see or visualize what you are doing right or wrong before you are able to improve.

My pictures are primarily of players just like yourself, the so-called "average" player, weekend player, and hacker. These players are much easier to relate to. At any rate, the top players don't necessarily have the strokes that you want to pattern yours after.

While writing this book I have learned more about myself, writing, and, yes, tennis, also. In tennis as in any other field the cliché holds true: you learn something new everyday—well, almost everyday!

I've written this book because I have seen so many aspects of the game presented incorrectly on the courts and in books and magazines. Some important aspects have not even been mentioned at all. One of my goals is to inform everyone of the benefits this game has to offer, and how rewarding it can be.

Now just because I have written a book on tennis does not mean I know everything there is to know about the sport. I am constantly learning. I don't think anyone knows all there is about anything. And if someone tells you they do, then that tells you what kind of person they are.

I have tried to present everything as clearly and simply as possible. I hope I will have answered many questions you might have about the game. Remember the game of tennis is only as easy or as hard as we make it. So keep it simple, and have more fun.

THE TENNIS DOCTOR

History

THE GAME OF TENNIS that we know and love so well today has only been in existence for a little over a hundred years, though variations of the sport date back centuries earlier. Actually the game of tennis was derived from a combination of several other games.

Though some of its history is still vague, the conclusion that most historians agree on is that the sport started as early as the fourteenth century in France. From what they have learned, the sport was first played in courtyards and resembled a game similar to handball. Even as early as the mid-fourteenth century, the sport was played inside as well as out. The game inside was referred to as "short tennis" and the outside game as "long tennis."

The early outdoor game consisted of hitting the ball with your hand covered with a glove. When the inside game became more popular, crude racquets were invented to extend one's reach. Tennis of this type was played for many years, and there were some instances when a player with a racquet played a player without one. Sounds like something Bobby Riggs might try!

During the early nineteenth century the game of "royal tennis" was played. This game was played on a court 110 feet by 38 feet, with a net height of 5 feet at the net posts. The game resembled racquetball in that the ball was played off the sloping sides surrounding the court.

Another game that had an impact on our modern game of tennis was "racquets." In this game players alternately hit the ball against a walled court. No net was used. The modern game of "squash" was derived from this game.

Even the game of badminton had an influence on tennis. Badminton was played as early as 1850.

The man most historians give credit to for inventing our modern game of tennis is Major Walter Clopton Wingfield. This 1873 game actually "took the principles of court tennis and adapted them to outdoor play where there were no walls. It was played on grass. The net from badminton was employed, the ball was borrowed from the 'fives' and the scoring technique was taken from 'racquets.' "* In

* *Official Encyclopedia of Tennis*, Harper & Row.

1

order to make the novelty his own so he could benefit financially, Wingfield called the invention "Sphairistike, or Lawn Tennis," from the ancient Greek game, and designed the shape of the court in the form of an hourglass, with a high net and winging on both sides. The hourglass court was 60 feet in length and at the widest part, the baseline, it was 30 feet in width. The shape of the court can be visualized by noting that even though the baseline was 30 feet in width, the net was only 21 feet wide. The net was low, 4 feet 8 inches at the center, but 7 feet at the sides. How would you have liked to play on a court like that? You would sure have to use a lot of top spin.

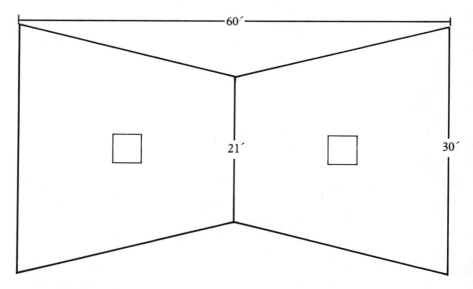

An Early Tennis Court

"A few months after the game of Spairistike was patented, the British garrison stationed in Bermuda obtained some sets of equipment. An American visitor, Mary Ewing Outerbridge, of Staten Island, New York, tried the game and became very interested in it. When she returned home in the spring of 1874 she brought with her a net, some balls, and several rackets that had been given to her by some of the British officers. Upon arriving at the port of New York, she had difficulty in getting her tennis set through customs house, as no one knew what it was, and consequently could not classify it for duty. But her brother, A. Emelius Outerbridge, was prominent

The Tennis Court

The parts and dimensions of the court you need to know.

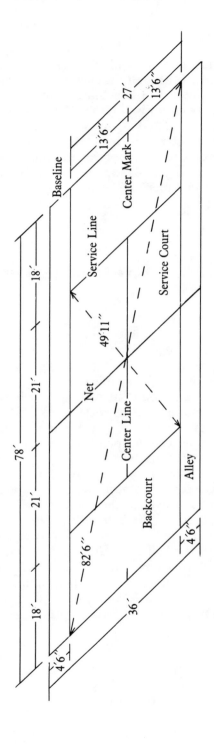

in shipping circles, and she called upon him for assistance, and he helped her get the set through the customs. Outerbridge was an active cricketer and a director of the Staten Island Cricket and Baseball Club, which had its grounds at Camp Washington (later St. George), Staten Island. He obtained permission from the Club to allow his sister shortly after her return from Bermuda to set up her net and mark out a court on one corner of the grounds. Most tennis historians agree this court on Staten Island, which was laid in 1874 was the first lawn tennis court in America."*

Basic Concepts of the Game

TENNIS IS A GAME OF MANY basic concepts and rules with which we need to become familiar. If we happen to forget one or more of these basic rules, then we get into trouble. You and I as players have problems when we try to think about more than one concept at a time. Our minds just aren't capable of handling it, at least mine isn't. When was the last time you tried patting your head and rubbing your stomach at the same time? See what I mean? So, while on the court direct all your thoughts toward one aspect at a time, such as hitting the ball at the proper contact point or following through. Then you shouldn't have as many problems.

Another basic concept, which most players tend to forget, is that the way the racquet face is pointing at point of contact, is the direction in which the ball will travel. If the racquet face is pointing down-the-line, that is the direction the ball will go, and we can't do anything about it. Unfortunately, you can't point your racquet face in one direction and wish the ball in a different direction. The basic laws of physics don't work that way. I know—I've tried! Wouldn't it be fun if they did! Just imagine how you could fool an opponent.

Here are some more basic concepts you need to be aware of before you can hope to improve your level of play:

1. Being relaxed.
2. Proper grip.
3. Good footwork—ready positions, stance.

* *Official Encyclopedia of Tennis*, Harper & Row, pages 1–8.

4

4. Concentrate on the ball.
5. Stroke development.
6. Timing.
7. Strategy.

These fundamentals have been listed according to their priority, which may surprise you and be different from yours. Most players when they're on the court usually think first about concentrating on watching the ball, their strokes, and what strategy they will use, if they have any. This may be fine for a few of you, however, the majority of us need to start with Step 1.

Being relaxed

When you step out on the court does it feel like home to you or does it feel like a foreign country? If it feels like home then you are relaxed.

Being relaxed on the court in my mind is the hardest single element of the game. The reason is that as players we put too much unnecessary pressure on ourselves. This pressure can be categorized by "the fear of losing" and the "fear of winning." If you are like nearly every player in the world, when you are out on the court playing a match, you are not out there just to have fun, you are out there to win. Right! These fears vary with every player, but don't let anyone fool you. They are real, and it is up to us to deal with them the best we can. How we handle these fears will be a big determining factor in the outcome of a match. If you are normal it is impossible to completely eliminate these fears. The fear of losing refers to not wanting to lose, and especially looking bad while doing so. You realize if you look too bad they may not want to play with you again. The fear of winning, which isn't as common, can be depicted as: what happens if I win? Now there will be more pressure on me to win again!

In order to eliminate some of the unwarranted pressure, you first have to put your own game into its proper perspective. You must first ask yourself these important questions. How good am I? What are my goals? Too often we think we are better than we really are, and this is where the problems originate. Once you can put your ability level in the proper frame of reference, then and only then will you be on your way to playing better tennis.

To help make yourself relax on the court, here are a few suggestions:

5

A. Take a deep breath before every point.

B. Shake your body to relax the muscles.

C. Tell yourself a good joke.

D. Concentrate totally on the ball.

E. Play often—the more you play the more relaxed you become.

Remember that of the millions of people that play tennis daily, half of them have to lose. So don't worry about it. You are not alone, and there is always tomorrow.

Proper grip

Your grip refers to the way in which you hold your racquet. To get the maximum out of your strokes, the grip you use needs to be compatible with them. The proper grip enables you to have the fatty part of your hand behind the stroke, which in turn will give you the control and power you desire. The various grips will be discussed in detail in the chapter on Grips and Spins.

Good footwork—ready positions, stance

You may have the best strokes in the world, but what good are they if you can't get into position to hit them? Good footwork begins with a good, moving, ready position. Your ability, as well as your opponent's, will dictate where this position is. This position on the court is sometimes referred to as a "home base." You have two home bases; one generally two to three feet behind the baseline, and the other one halfway between the net and the service line. When I was first learning to play, the home base at the net was a racquet's length away from the net. It has since been moved back to give ample time to react to the ball, enough room to get a good step forward for your volleys, and make it easier to cover the lob.

The depth on your opponent's shots is the determining factor as to where you position yourself in the backcourt. Obviously, the more depth on the ball the farther back you need to play. Avoid standing too close to the baseline for this will make it too difficult to hit balls that land near the baseline. It would be like hitting half volleys from there. Remember it is always easier to move forward for a ball than it is to move backward. If these are not the best home bases for your style of game, be flexible enough to adjust accordingly. After rallying for a while this position should be established.

Sometime while watching a professional tennis match, observe what the players are doing between strokes while the ball is in play. You will see they seem to be in perpetual motion, constantly on the move. This motion speeds up your adrenalin, which in turn makes you react faster and move more quickly. Tracy Austin is a great example to watch. I would swear she has a little motor inside her. She is constantly on the go. This type of movement is often referred to as "unwaiting." This motion is usually in the form of a bouncing action.

The following are some fundamentals needed for a good, moving ready position.

1. Stay relaxed.
2. Concentrate on the ball.
3. Stay on the balls of your feet, which are located just behind your toes. This will enable you to move more quickly. As in all sports, you don't want to be caught flatfooted.
4. Your racquet should be held loosely in your preferred grip. The forehand grip has been the general rule, however, for some players, it is easier to change from a backhand to a forehand grip. Find out which way is best for you.
5. Your racquet should be held low, about waist high if you are at the baseline and if you use the straight backswing style.
6. Your racquet should be held slightly higher if you are at your home base near the net, or if you use a looping style of swing from the baseline.
7. Your knees should be slightly bent, for quicker movements.
8. Your racquet should be pointed straight ahead.
9. Unwait or bounce between strokes.
10. When you find yourself out of position after returning a ball, return immediately to your nearest home base.
11. When playing at the net shift your home base slightly toward the direction of the ball.
12. When rallying from the baseline, if you are pulled wide, try to get back to the center of the court before your opponent makes contact with the ball. That way you will be in position for the next shot.
13. Get stopped before hitting the shot.

Your footwork should consist of quick, normal-sized steps, with your first step being the most important. Just like a sprinter coming out of the starting blocks, you want to explode to the ball. Be sure to run on the balls of your feet which, besides giving you better balance, enables you to run faster.

Your steps should be precise, making it possible to get into correct position to hit the ball. If you are either too close or too far away from the ball, you will lose all your control and power. The correct distance from the ball can best be illustrated by hitting a ball while holding another ball between your arm and side just below your arm pit. If you are too far away from the ball, the ball under your arm will fall out before contact is made. And if you are too close to the ball you will either hit your leg with your racquet or use the infamous "scooping stroke," which should only be used with a shovel. In other words, you want to be a comfortable distance from the ball.

This is the classic ready position behind the baseline.

This is the classic ready position at the net. Note that racquet is higher at net than it is at baseline if you are not using a loop swing.

Make the "contact point" for your back hand at least one foot in front of your lead foot as demonstrated here.

The proper contact point for your forehand is even with your leading or front foot.

This demonstrates the "hitting zone." It is important that you keep the racquet in this path throughout your forehand swing.

The "open" stance.

Have you ever experienced the "wall syndrome"? This player demonstrates a typical example. After making contact with the ball, the racquet seems to stop prematurely, as though it had hit an imaginary wall.

This player demonstrates what you might look like if you are late hitting your forehand.

Ever feel as though your arms aren't long enough for a particular stroke? Chances are your problem lies in inadequate foot work. You do not need an arm extender. This player shows what it means to be overextended.

This player demonstrates a very common mistake: he is taking too large a backswing.

Ever look up to admire your winner only to find it in the net? This player shows how you look when you anticipate a shot.

These pictures show what you may look like when you over run a ball or are too tired to move out of the way. When you are forced into a scoop-shot, you lose control and power.

With some practice and knowledge, you can learn to anticipate where the ball is going before your opponent makes contact with the ball. Anticipating is knowing, or at least having a good idea, where the ball will be hit to. This knowledge will give you a distinct advantage over your opponent.

Here are some thoughts to keep in mind which will help you to anticipate better:

1. Know your opponent's strength and weakness.
2. Know your own game and abilities.
3. Know the percentages.
4. Have a knowledge of the basic strategies.
5. Don't anticipate too early, otherwise your opponent will have time to adjust his stroke and hit the ball to the open area of the court.

Moving correctly and knowing where to be in singles or doubles will improve the average player's game 50 percent. If you remember nothing else about good footwork, remember there is no substitute for hustle. "Hustling," trying for every ball, will win you more matches than you can imagine.

There are two basic stances used in tennis, the "open" and "closed" stances. The open stance refers to hitting the ball with your stomach or navel facing the net. This type of stance occurs when either you are out of position, or on clay and grass courts when sliding for the ball. In either case, unless you are very strong, the result will be a weaker shot since you will only be using your arm muscles to stroke the ball.

A closed stance refers to hitting the ball with your side to the net. This is the preferred style because you can get your entire body behind your stroke making it much easier to hit, and giving you the desired control and power.

Concentrate on the ball

Concentrating totally on the ball is not an easy aspect, not even for the pros. In fact, there aren't any easy parts to the game. If there were, we would all be going to the U.S. Open next year, and not to be spectators. Unfortunately we all concentrate on watching the ball to some degree, but not well enough or long enough. Dr. Leon Revien in his book *Sports Vision* has stated that the average person utilizes only 30 to 40 percent of their visual potential. So there is plenty of room for improvement, and it can happen by just taking a little time to conduct your own eye improvement program. For more information on such a program, I would recommend finding his book in your local book store.

To watch the ball completely, its velocity, direction, and spin, we must watch it all the time, and not just when it's on our side of the net. We must concentrate on the ball throughout its total flight, and while it's making contact with your opponent's racquet as well as your own. As you have heard before, you will not actually see the ball hit your strings. Instead, you will see a yellow or white blur. Our eyes just can't focus that well, that quickly. Studies have shown that the ball stays on our strings for just three milliseconds. In comparison, this is faster than you can blink your eyes.

I'm sure most of you, at one time or another, have had the common problem of being unable to fall asleep at night. As simple as it is some nights, other nights it takes hours to get to "dreamland." The reason is that we simply have too many things and ideas dancing around in our minds. Remember our minds are not computers. They can only handle one idea or problem at a time. So whether you are trying to fall asleep or hit a solid backhand, just concentrate on *one* element at a time.

Concentrating on the ball is not natural, but it can be improved by practicing a few simple techniques and blocking everything else out of your mind. These techniques and theories are:

1. Use the bounce-hit technique. When the ball bounces, say to yourself "bounce," and when you make contact with the ball, say "hit."
2. Watch the arc the flight of the ball makes.
3. Look for the writing on the ball or the seams.
4. Keep your head still while watching the ball and throughout the stroke. Follow the ball with only your eyes.
5. Keep your head either up or down, depending on the stroke, until you *hear* the ball hit your strings.
6. When you make contact with the ball, have your head on the same level or plane as the ball. However, this can't be done with the serve or overhead.
7. Try *not* to see the ball you hit cross the net. In other words, don't look up too early.
8. After you make contact with the ball, freeze for a second and hold your follow-through. Don't rush to get ready for the next shot.

9. Convince yourself that the ball is your opponent and play the ball, *not* your opponent.
10. Why look up early? Your opponent can't hurt you while the ball is on your side of the net.

Just like everything else you do in life, your mental aspect has a lot to do with the total outcome. Two players on the professional tour that exhibit great mental and emotional control are Bjorn Borg and Chris Evert Lloyd. They have only one thing on their minds and they let nothing affect or get in the way of their goal, which is to be the best in the world at what they do. You and I, on the other hand, have trouble with this aspect. We are usually thinking too much about what to fix for dinner, or whether or not our big oil deal has come through.

In order to play the tennis we are capable of playing, our mind and body need to be in perfect harmony with each other. They need to work together smoothly and efficiently like a fine-tuned engine.

Stroke development

Once you have distinguished the direction in which the ball is going, immediately pivot or turn your feet in the direction of the ball, while at the same time taking your racquet back. You might say your foot-work and backswing go hand in hand. Just turning your side to the net brings your racquet half way back, so all you really have to do is take it back a little farther. Your ultimate goal is to have your racquet back into position *before* the ball crosses onto your side of the court. That way you will have to wait for the ball, which will enable you to take a nice smooth stroke instead of being rushed. Now the butt of your racquet will be pointing to the net. For you mathematically inclined players, the total movement from your ready position to the end of your follow-through should be 360 degrees. In other words, your racquet moves from directly in front of you to directly behind you in your backswing; your forward swing finishes out in front of you and above your head. Any larger swing is unnecessary and, for the average player, takes too long. Many players elongate their swing and then wonder why they are always late hitting the ball, or why they don't have the control and power they desire.

The 360° Theory

Timing

Timing refers to making contact with the ball, at the proper spot in relationship to your body, at the precisely correct split second. You probably are asking yourself, *When is the appropriate time to start my foreward swing?* That's a very good question. The answer depends on the speed of the ball, and how fast you react to it. This is where hitting countless thousands of balls comes into play. That is what it will take before you are able to groove your strokes and be able to consistently meet the ball at the proper "contact point." And this is what it will take in order to hit the solid shots you want. Your contact point will vary depending on the stroke you are hitting. These specific contact points will be discussed in detail with the appropriate stroke.

After contact with the ball is made, it is important to continue your forward swing in the direction you intend the ball to go. This continuing path that the racquet takes is referred to as the "hitting zone" or "power zone." This zone actually begins once you drop your racquet into position on your backswing and extends through your follow-through. If you keep your racquet in this zone or path throughout your forward swing, it will give you the control and power you need.

Any deviation from this path will cause you to lose that control and power. Two main alterations occur if you either abruptly point the tip of your racquet on your follow-through or swing across the hitting zone.

Your follow-through is just as important as any other part of your stroke. Without the proper follow-through you will lose control and power on the stroke. A smooth, long follow-through shows that you are relaxed and didn't stop your stroke prematurely.

Your follow-through should always be in the direction in which you intend the ball to go. You should finish either above your head or about waist high, depending on the type of spin you put on the ball. Too often I see players prematurely stop their follow-through as if their racquet just hit a wall, or they lengthen it in such a manner that it looks like they are trying to strangle themselves. In either case, the result is the same—a poor shot. Your follow-through, when using top spin, should finish with your racquet face slightly directed toward the sky and above your head. When using underspin, your racquet face will remain slightly open or beveled to the sky throughout the stroke.

When observing beginners or even veteran players, I have found that they are more concerned with just getting the ball back any way they can rather than using the proper stroke technique. Even though stroke development is near the bottom on your list of priorities, it is still vitally important. If you constantly practice just getting the ball back, how do you expect to get good strokes and improve your game?

It is equally important *not* to practice poor stroking techniques that develop bad habits, which are hard to break. This is why it is easier sometimes to work with a raw beginner than a player already set in his ways.

If a beginner or any other player is having problems with a particular stroke, I recommend practice, practice, and more practice on strokes for a while. Don't worry where the ball goes. I realize it is easier said than done, but you should be more concerned about how your stroke feels and looks. If your stroke feels and looks good, the ball will be going where you want it to.

Most of us don't take advantage of the invention of the ball machine or the backboard. They are two of the best ways of grooving and refining our strokes.

Strategy

The type of strategy you use is the last of the fundamentals or priorities, because the best strategy in the world won't help if you can't accomplish the first six fundamentals. Your strategy on the court is only as good as your ability to execute one stroke at a time. The various strategies will be discussed later in their own chapter.

Crucial points

If winning is the name of the game, and, for most of us it is, then don't fool yourself by thinking some points aren't critical. All points are critical. It's just that some are slightly more critical than others. The most critical point is the last one, that's the one we're always trying to win. Otherwise the most important points are the break and game points. These are the points that separate the winners from losers. I've done this, and I'm sure many of you have, also—won more total points than my opponent but ended up losing the match—I lost the "big" points. When this happens it should tell you that you are not "tournament tough," and you need to play more matches. It has

20

been said that John McEnroe plays all points the same, trying to win every single point. That's one of the reasons he is one of the best, if not the best, player in the world. He never lets up, and neither should you. How often has this happened to you: you are up a service break, cruising along, when you start to lose your concentration and play a few loose or poorly played points? In just a matter of minutes, the "momentum" has changed sides and you have lost the next game, set, and match.

Play each point as if it is the most important one of your life, because it just might be. Never give up on a point. Try to run all balls down. If you don't get to one the first time you probably will the next time. This also shows your opponent what great shape you are in. He will see that he can't wear you down. It might just give you a mental edge.

Tennis as a Supplementary Sport

I RECOMMEND THAT COACHES and athletes of other sports use tennis as a form of supplementary training. It would be especially good for the so-called "big men" players in football and basketball. Too often, especially in high school, you see some big young men who are unable to play up to their potential because they are physically unable to handle their size.

The game of tennis will help these athletes live up to their potential by improving their:

1. Eye–hand coordination.
2. Quickness.
3. Reflexes.
4. Endurance.
5. Agility.
6. Sportsmanship.
7. Mental ability.

Tennis will help everyone in these areas, even nonathletic people.

Professional football teams have already learned the benefits from racquet sports, and now many teams have their own racquet ball facilities in their training camps.

21

Nutrition

I DON'T RECOMMEND any special diet as far as tennis is concerned. From my research I have found that most players before a match prefer to eat a well-balanced meal that contains plenty of carbohydrates, food with starch in it.

Keeping in mind that I am not a nutrition specialist, I also feel it is important to take *one* multipurpose vitamin and a vitamin C tablet, since unfortunately we don't always eat the way we should.

My personal feeling, which may vary from yours, is that there is no possible way smoking anything can be good for you, and I know for a fact it will only harm your tennis performance. Though smoking probably affects you in other ways as well, I know it limits the endurance that you need for a match. And, if you're looking for another excuse for why you got tired and lost, this one is as good as any.

As far as losing weight, I feel you should still eat a well balanced meal, but in smaller quantities. As far as I am concerned, the only way to lose weight sensibly is to burn off more calories than you consume, by tennis or any other form of exercise. Losing weight, unfortunately, is a slow and hard process, one that requires much willpower, determination, and time.

How Tennis Is Changing

IF YOU HEAR SOMEONE SAY the game of tennis or the way it is taught hasn't changed, that person doesn't know very much about the game. Some of the aspects that have changed are:

1. More strokes are being discussed, such as the lob volley and the return of the lob.
2. The training methods have improved.
3. The teaching methods have become more intense.

4. The stroking mechanics have changed due to the playing styles of popular players.
5. Strategy is becoming more advanced.
6. Students learn how the body affects the strokes.
7. Supplementary training techniques, such as weight training, are used.

You can see that nearly all phases of the game have been studied, analyzed, reevaluated, and improved upon for the advancement of the game.

Adverse Conditions

IF YOU ARE LIKE ME, you probably don't like to play tennis if it is very windy outside. Wind can have a big effect on you if you don't know how to compensate for it.

Playing in the wind is more of a mental adjustment than a physical one. There is nothing you can do about it, except for playing indoors or not playing, so don't worry about it and concentrate on the ball. Due to the strange effect the wind can have on the ball, you need to pay very close attention to it. Remember your opponent probably doesn't like playing in the wind either, and it is affecting him, also. The winner is usually the one who can best adjust his mind and game to the weather conditions.

Your serve and overhead will be the most affected by the wind. If your toss is higher than it should be, once the wind catches it, who knows what county it will come down in? So, if you do have one of those moon-ball tosses, lower it to the proper height, which is as high as you can reach. On your overheads let your lobs bounce first before hitting the ball. Overheads can be tricky enough on a calm day, let alone a windy one. Aim your ground strokes and lobs down the middle of the court, allowing plenty of room for error once the wind catches the ball. If it is just too windy to continue playing, play some mini-tennis. The wind won't have much effect on the ball, and you can still get some good exercise while practicing some of your strokes and fundamentals.

Believe it or not, some players like to play in the wind. That way they have an excuse if they lose. Don't be one of these players, this is not the attitude to take.

Whenever you play outdoors, the sun will usually be a factor. Fortunately, tennis courts are laid out facing north and south, so supposedly you never have to look directly into the sun. I wish the sun knew that. The sun can be one of your opponents if you don't know how to deal with it.

Just like with the wind, the sun is more of a mental adjustment than a physical one. The sun will only affect your serve and overhead. With both strokes you can use your opposite hand to shield your eyes from the sun. You may also need to make a slight adjustment with your body by turning it away from the direct rays of the sun. Again, I would recommend letting the ball bounce first on the overhead. That way the sun won't affect you too much. A good strategy when playing on a sunny day is to lob more when your opponent is facing the sun. I know this is mean but it works.

Ball Pickup Techniques

EVEN BEFORE A PLAYER hits a ball you can tell how good he or she is by the way he or she picks up balls from the court. So when scouting a player, watch to see which method he uses. Once you have perfected the advanced technique you will be ready to psych your opponent out—at least until you hit the ball.

The four techniques are:

1. An A player will gracefully bend at the knees, bend down, and place the racquet on top of the ball. Then a quick wrist snap will bounce the ball up.
2. A B player brings the ball next to his foot and simultaneously lifts his foot and racquet, lifting the ball up to where he can get his racquet under it.
3. C players and others bend their knees, bend down, and pick up the ball with their hands.

Tournament players let the ball persons do this menial task. Which style do you use?

Beginners

TO CHANGE AN OLD PHRASE: "To begin or not to begin, that is the question." This is what each of us asked ourselves before we undertook this sport. To be a beginner is not a sin, or even as bad a position to be in as one might imagine. When you're at the bottom there's no place to go but up. Remember, you may be a beginner in tennis, but you are advanced in other fields.

Too often we more advanced players forget we were once beginners ourselves. Beginners should not be looked down on, but rather commended for their effort in trying to improve themselves and their game. This is especially true for you middle-aged beginners. I, for one, realize how hard it is to take up a new sport after our "prime."

Advanced players take note, these beginners won't be beginners for long, so watch out. The are out to beat you!

Beginners should be encouraged and helped, not ridiculed and shied away from, as if they had the bubonic plague. They will improve immensely with just some positive encouragement and reinforcement. If you see a beginner out on the court looking "lost," please give him some of your knowledge. While you will be helping him, you will also be making yourself feel good inside. Remember, someone did it for you once.

Help them by giving them just one or two new concepts to think about. Any more will jumble their minds. When teaching a beginner be very careful, especially if it is a relative, not to expect too much at first. It might be harder for them than it was for you.

Before you even go out on the court, practice some eye–hand coordination drills first, along with some mirror tennis. This way they can get a feel for the game before they even get to the court. Once out on the court gently throw balls for them to hit. This will make it easier for them, so they can groove their strokes. Then try some mini-tennis. After they have accomplished that, gradually move your way back to the baseline hitting easy and letting them move you around. While hitting with a beginner, work on your placement and patience. You will find this experience rewarding, and you will realize that playing with a beginner can even be fun.

Keeping Score

YOU'RE PROBABLY ASKING YOURSELF where did they ever come up with a scoring system like this? Ever since the earliest days of tennis, the scoring has used the number fifteen as a scoring unit. As early as the sixteenth century each point was awarded a score of fifteen. The scoring then went fifteen for the first point, thirty for the second point, and forty-five the third. Then, as today, one more point was needed to win the game, or, if the score reached forty-five all or deuce, two more consecutive points were needed to win the game. Tennis historians cannot agree on any definite reason for the fifteen scoring system. A fairly common assumption among historians is that the unit of fifteen was taken from a unit of measure used at that time.

The only two changes in scoring over the centuries has been to change the score forty-five to forty. The belief is that by making it shorter, it was easier to call the score. I, for one, just think they were trying to confuse us more. The other change was from having to win four games to win a set; we now have to win six games for a set. The six-game set revision was instituted back in the early 1700s.

In both singles and doubles the server, along with his other responsibilities, is the scorekeeper. This in itself is a major responsibility and must not be taken lightly. Call out the score loud enough so each player can hear you before each point. This way you shouldn't lose track of the score, but, if you do, don't worry about it—the other players will help you out. Remember you always say *your* score first.

Before the start of each game the score is "love" "love." The score "love" denotes *no* points. Some romanticist must have thought that up. The first point you win is referred to as "15." The second point is "30." The third point is "40." And the fourth and possibly final point is "game." So conceivably you can win a game by winning only four points. Sounds easy doesn't it? However, if the score reaches 40–40, it is more commonly referred to as "deuce." Deuce is only deuce when each player has three points. Too often I hear players call out "30 deuce." The score may be tied at 30–all, but technically the score is *not* deuce. Once the score has reached deuce, you must win *two* consecutive points in order to win the game.

The first point after deuce is called either "advantage in" or "advantage out" depending on who won this point. "Advantage in" or "ad in" as it is more commonly called, denotes the server or server's team as winning that point. "Advantage out" or "ad out" refers to the receiver or receiver's team as winning the point. The advantage part makes sense, but I wish I knew where they got the "in" and "out."

Scoring in tennis

1. The server's score is always called first.
2. Points are scored as follows:

> No points—Love
> First point—15
> Second point—30
> Third point—40
> Fourth point—Game

> Deuce—each side has three points. One side must now win two consecutive points to win the game.

> Advantage—the first point after deuce.

> a. If the server wins the first point after deuce, the score is called Advantage (Ad) In.

> b. If the receiver wins the first point after deuce, the score is called Advantage (Ad) Out.

A set consists of winning at least six games by a two game margin. If the score of any set reaches five games all, then a player or team will have to win the next two games, to win the set. If the game score reaches six games all, then one of a number of tie breakers can be used to see who wins the set.

Player A Server wins	Player B Receiver wins	Score
1 point	0 point	15–Love
2 points	0 point	30–Love
3 points	0 point	40–Love
3 points	1 point	40–15
3 points	2 points	40–30
1 point	1 point	15–All
2 points	2 points	30–All
3 points	3 points	Deuce
4 points	3 points	Ad In
3 points	4 points	Ad Out
5 points	3 points	GAME— player A

27

A match usually consists of winning two out of three sets. However, some tournaments are played for the best three out of five sets.

There is another type of scoring system. This is the type that was used when World Team Tennis was played. It is a simpler form, though it puts more pressure on the players, since there is no advantage in or advantage out. The scoring goes as follows: one, two, three, and game. If the score reaches three–all, the receiver gets his choice of where to receive the serve. Whoever wins that point wins the game. This scoring system is referred to as the No-Ad Scoring System.

Tie Breakers

IN MOST TOURNAMENTS TODAY you will find some type of "tie breaker" scoring system used if a set reaches six games all. The term "tie breaker" comes from its definition—to break a tie. The two most popular ones are the 9-point tie breaker and the 12-point tie breaker.

Tie breaker—12-point

In a 12-point play-off, players take two serves each, changing sides after the sixth point, or split the first two serves and then continue the two-serve format. The first player to win 7 points in the series wins the set or match.

If the score reaches 6–all in a play off, the players can agree to another 12-point play-off, or alternate serves until one player has won two consecutive points. Alternating serves are best known as a "lingering death" play-off.

If a second set must be decided in a play-off, the player who served the first two points in the initial tie breaker now will serve second in the series.

Sudden death—9-point

"Sudden death" is the term that has been used to describe the 9-point tie breaker. It follows the same basic pattern as a 12-point play-off.

Player A serves points 1 and 2, left and right court; then B serves points 3 and 4 in the same pattern. Players change sides. Player A serves 5 and 6. B then serves points 7 and 8. If neither has earned 5 points, B serves point 9, and the receiver has the choice of receiving left or right court.

In almost all cases, scoring for tie breakers from sets at 6–all is 7–6. Doubles follows the same format. Each player serves from the same end of the court that he served from during that particular set.

The Rules of the Game

IT IS IMPORTANT THAT YOU completely understand the rules of the game. Knowing these rules will make tennis more enjoyable, and enable you to use your skills to their fullest advantage. The basic rules have changed considerably since Major Walter Clopton Wingfield, developed the first set of rules in 1874.

Besides the hourglass shape of the court used then, a small box was located in the middle of each court. From this position the server served the ball making it land behind his opponent's box. The receiver could either return the ball as a volley or after the first bounce. The scoring system used then was similar to our modern day scoring used in badminton. The server could *only* win points, and he needed 15 points to win a game.

The following are just some of the basic modern day rules of tennis that you should be familiar with:

1. The height of the net in the middle is 3 feet and at the net posts it is 3 feet 6 inches.
2. The ball can bounce no more than one time on each side of the court, otherwise the point will be lost.
3. The ball can only be hit once on each side.
4. It is illegal to "carry" the ball, which involves holding the ball on the strings longer than normal. This usually happens when you catch the ball behind you or too far to one side. The result is that you end up throwing the ball back rather than hitting it.
5. When choosing who will serve and receive, the winner of the spin of the racquet actually has *three* choices:

a. Choose either to serve or receive.

b. Choose which side of the court to take.

c. Choose to have his opponent make the decision. This is a move in reverse psychology that makes your opponent wonder what's up.

6. When delivering serve you alternate serving to the right and left courts, always beginning from the right.

7. If any ball strikes a line within the proper court, the ball is good. Even if the ball is more out than on the line, it is still good. Remember in calling the close balls, if you can't see the ball completely out, then it must be good.

8. A service let occurs anytime the ball strikes the net, or any part of the net, before it touches the court and lands within the proper service court. When this happens, the serve is replayed.

9. If the server serves and the receiver is not ready and does not make an attempt to return the serve, a let should be played.

10. When playing either singles or doubles, you alternate sides of the court after the odd number of total games, such as 1, 3, 5, and so forth.

11. If you discover that someone has served out of turn, the proper server should serve immediately, but all points scored and any faults shall be reckoned. However, if a game has been completed before the mistake was discovered, the order of service remains as altered.

12. An error made in receiving order, when discovered, shall remain as altered until the end of the game. When the next receiving game begins the original order is resumed.

13. If the server hits his partner with the serve in doubles it is a fault. Also you may lose your partner.

14. The order of service should be decided at the beginning of each set and shall remain the same throughout the set. However, the order can be changed at the beginning of each additional set. The same rule applies for receiving serve.

15. You can serve underhand as long as you don't bounce the ball during the serve.

16. A let is an interruption of play during a point. It should be decided before play begins what will be considered a let. Such a case would be if a ball rolls onto your court from another court. If a let occurs during a serve, only that one serve shall be replayed. If it happens during a point, the point will be replayed.

17. Often when you're out on the court for a match you will hear a player say, "Let's play first serve in." In most cases these players haven't taken the necessary time to warm up their serves. Shoulder injuries can occur as a result. If someone says this to you, your reply should be, "First return in." The server has an advantage already, let's not give him a greater one.

I recommend either reading up on all the rules or purchasing a book with the entire set of rules included.

Code of Ethics

THE CODE OF ETHICS consists of the unwritten rules governing your behavior, or sportsmanship if you will, on the court. These rules should be taken seriously and adhered to. They will make your playing more enjoyable, and may even help to improve your game.

1. Set a good example, be a model for the young players.
2. Call the balls on your side of the court only, unless your opponent asks for help.
3. Control your temper. In most cases a bad temper will only cause hard feelings and ruin your concentration.
4. Don't throw your racquet. It is an expensive piece of equipment.
5. If you don't know your opponent introduce yourself.
6. After the match shake hands with your opponent.
7. When making a call "out" yell it and point the direction of the error in case your opponent didn't hear the call.
8. If your ball rolls onto an adjacent court, wait until play has stopped before retrieving your ball.
9. Don't stall.
10. Don't ask spectators to make a call.
11. Don't make any unnecessary noises or distracting movements during play.
12. Wait for your opponent to be ready before starting the point.
13. Wear the proper attire.
14. If there are players waiting for a court play only your allotted time, usually one hour.

31

Mini- or Short-Court Tennis

MINI- OR SHORT-COURT TENNIS IS probably the best kept secret of tennis, and for this reason also the least used. This is a game as well as a practice technique played within the service lines. Mini-tennis is primarily used as a warm-up drill. It is a good way to warm up the body as well as the eyes. Within five to ten minutes you should be ready to progress your way back to the baseline. Besides warming up, this game helps in developing your:

1. Footwork.
2. Return of serve.
3. Approach shots.
4. Dropshots.
5. Angle shots.
6. Drop volleys.
7. Consistency.
8. Placement.
9. Conditioning.

Mini- or short-court tennis varies from regular tennis in that:

1. You use a shorter backswing, but a normal follow-through for control because you are closer to the net.
2. Your home base is two to three feet behind the service line.
3. Volleys may or may not be permitted.
4. You serve underhand, bouncing the ball first.

This is an especially good learning drill for beginners, and at the same time can be a challenging game for more advanced players. As you will find out, if you don't already know, this game takes more skill than you think. To judge your own ability, see how long you can keep the ball in play. Set yourself some goals, one hundred hits apiece is not unrealistic. Remember if you can't control the ball here, how can you expect to control it using the full court?

32

Mirror Tennis

MIRROR TENNIS IS A TRAINING and learning technique guaranteed to improve your tennis game if practiced regularly. Boxers for many years have used a similar training practice, "shadow boxing," for basically the same purposes: loosening up and practicing delivering punches in the proper fashion. Don't let the name deceive you. A mirror is not required to make this practice possible, it just helps.

The reasons for using this seldom used learning aid are:

1. To instill in your mind a picture of what your strokes look like.
2. To see any flaws in your strokes and correct them.
3. To practice your strokes so that you can get a feeling for them. You should be able to tell if a stroke is good or bad just by the way it feels.
4. By practicing your strokes over and over your muscles become aware of what they should be doing and this awareness is called "muscle memory."
5. It is a very good warm-up exercise. This can be another good way to prevent injuries.

Mirror tennis is one exercise that does not take very long. Five to ten minutes is plenty of time to cover all your strokes and to get warmed up. Using a little imagination you can get a good work-out and have some fun at the same time.

During this warm-up exercise try closing your eyes at various stages of your strokes and say exactly what position your racquet is in in relationship to your body. This is one basic skill you need in perfecting your strokes. You can practice your footwork, as well as your ball toss. You can take your footwork drill one step further and go through some movement drills, such as serve and rush and return of serve and rush.

33

Warming-Up

BEFORE YOU PUT ONE FOOT on the court your warm-up should already have begun. Prior to warming up on the court your mind and muscles should be ready to go. Your mental preparation may consist of thinking and picturing in your mind your strokes, what you would do in a particular situation, and basically just getting into the right frame of mind by shutting out all possible distractions.

In order to prevent possible injuries, flexibility exercises are a must. They will only take about five minutes, and they can be the most important minutes of your warm-up. Some flexibility exercises are discussed in this book. I would also recommend that you practice your strokes off the court, possibly using the mirror tennis concept.

Since court warm-up time is relatively short—five to ten minutes, and even less during the indoor season when court time and costs are at a premium—it is important to make the most of it.

Mini-tennis is the *best* way to start your warm-up. You need to stay in the forecourt just a minute or two. Then gradually work your way back to the baseline. Warm-up on the court should consist of warming up all the strokes you will use in the course of the match. This includes: dropshots, overheads, drop volleys, and approach shots. Due to the importance of the second serve it should not be neglected during this time.

In either singles or doubles, it is best to warm everyone's serves at the same time. Besides taking less time it is also a more organized approach. At the same time you can be practicing your return of serve, which can always use some work.

Depending on how often you practice, this may be the only practice time you get between matches. For this reason game situations are not the time to be warming up your strokes, it should be done beforehand.

This time should also be used to scout your opponent. Find out his strengths, so you can try to avoid them, and his weaknesses, so you can exploit them.

Grips and Spins

YOUR GRIP AND THE TYPE of spin you put on the ball are interrelated. They work together to give you the type of stroke you desire. The way in which you hold your racquet will determine the type of spin on the ball.

It is important to your game to be familiar with the various types of grips and spins, and how they affect each other. It is a good idea and fun to experiment with the different grips and spins to see what they can do, and to find the right combination for you. If you are having a problem with a stroke, this just might be what's wrong.

Seldom will you find two players with the exact overall grip. When deciding on a grip, first look for comfort. A comfortable grip means confidence in a stroke, and that means a good stroke. Sometimes you may need to change your grip in order to improve your stroke. This can be one of the hardest things you will ever have to do in terms of tennis. It will take time to get used to the change, but stay with it because when you do it will pay off. Practice on and off the court. While you watch television practice changing grips or getting used to a new one. See how fast you can change them.

In addition to being comfortable, a grip should also be fairly firm. Your grip only needs to be tight enough to hold your racquet, not so tight that it cuts off the circulation in your arm. If you hold your racquet too tight, besides getting a tired and sore arm, you can't be relaxed, one of the key ingredients of the game.

With all grips the handle of your racquet should not extend below the base of your hand. When it does there is a tendency to use too much wrist action. This action will cause you to lose control of the ball. However, if you are looking for more spin or more wrist snap on your serve, this might be advisable. Also on all grips, your fingers should be comfortably spread apart.

There are three basic grips in tennis: eastern—used for forehands, backhands, and volleys; continental—used for volleys, serving, and occasionally ground strokes; and the western forehand. The eastern grips are generally preferred for the forehands, and backhands, due to the fact that you get more of your hand behind the racquet. This gives you more control and power while at the same time makes it easier to apply spin.

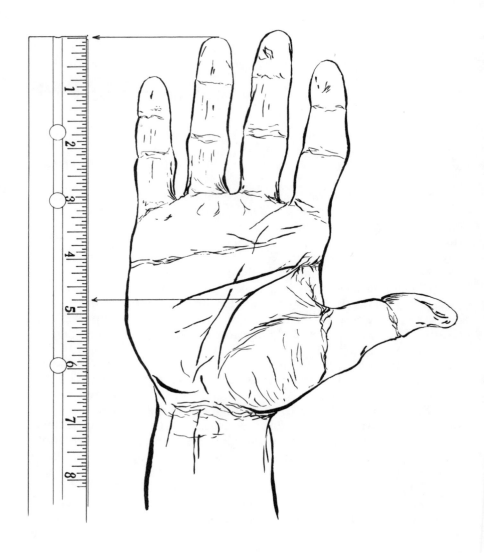

Finding Your Proper Grip Size

One rule for finding your grip size is to measure the distance from the tip of your ring finger to the middle crease of the "life-line" in the palm of your hand. This measurement should be the same as the distance around your grip. Another rule is that you should be able to place a finger comfortably between the butt of your racquet and your fingers. These are the two key ways of finding your proper grip size, but comfort is the main ingredient that will increase the effectiveness of your strokes.

To locate your eastern forehand grip:

1. Pretend you are shaking hands with the racquet. This was once called the "shaking hands grip." This method will bring you close to the correct grip. Since variations occur with grips while shaking hands, this expression is not used as much today.

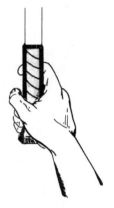

Eastern Forehand

2. A "v" is formed between your thumb and index finger on or slightly to the right of the top of your racquet grip.
3. Your palm is on the side of your grip.

To find your eastern backhand grip:

1. It is generally referred to as a quarter of a turn counterclockwise, or to the left of your eastern forehand grip. This grip will vary slightly depending upon where your eastern forehand grip is.

Eastern Backhand

2. The "v" is now located, depending on the type of handle your racquet has since they also vary, on the first or second bevel to the left.
3. Your palm will then be located on the top of the racquet grip.

The continental grip is used by players who don't want to, don't think they have time to, or have trouble changing grips. Tests have recently proven that it takes no longer to change grips than not to change them. However, this is the preferred grip by many players at the net, since it makes for one less aspect to worry about, especially in quick exchanges. This is the primary grip for serving because it enables you to put more spin on the ball, and makes it easier to snap your wrist. The continental grip can be used in the backcourt, but it is not advised. The continental grip is located between your eastern forehand and eastern backhand grips.

Continental

Western

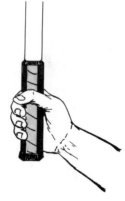

The western forehand grip is only recommended for players with more than average ability. The reason for a western grip is to produce excessive top spin. It will take hours of practice to get used to this grip. You will find a lot of balls at first will be mis-hits, due to the difficulty of this grip, and the timing involved. Even if you don't plan to use it, try it anyway and see what it feels like. Imagine you are Bjorn Borg!

To locate the western grip:

1. The "v" is located on the side of your grip about three bevels down.
2. The palm of your hand is below the racquet grip facing up.

Spin

SPIN IS SIMPLY THE ROTATION of the ball in flight. It is caused by the angle of your racquet at contact, and the path of your swing. Without any type of spin the ball is hit "flat" and has a tendency to float, usually out of the court. You can hit a flat ball harder, but you sacrifice the two most important ingredients—control and margin of error. There is little room for error on a flat shot. You should know when to use spin and which type to use, because it will make a difference.

Top Spin

TOP SPIN IS CLASSIFIED AS the foreward revolving motion of the ball in a clockwise direction. Top spin has probably been around since the game originated and was used by a few great pros as early as the 1940s, but has really come into its own due to the playing styles of Bjorn Borg and Guillermo Vilas.

When hitting a top spin shot you use a brushing action, brushing up the backside of the ball with the racquet. This action will cause the ball to stay on the strings a fraction of a second longer than normal. and this fraction of a second is what produces more control and spin.

Racquet Angles

It is extremely important that you be aware of the position of your racquet face when you make contact with the ball. No matter what type of swing you use, the racquet face must be in the correct position on contact or the ball will not go where you want it to go. Here are three basic racquet angles and the types of strokes they are used for.

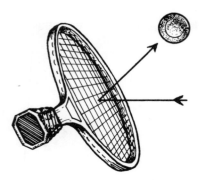

Open Racquet Face—Lobs

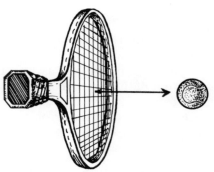

Flat Racquet Face—Flat or Top Spin Balls

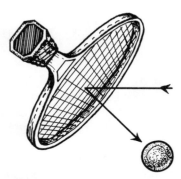

Closed Racquet Face—Underspin

This type of stroke will produce a ball that bounces higher than normal making it more difficult to return. You should be able to hear the difference between a top spin shot or, for that matter, any type of spin shot, and your typical flat shot. The sound will be that of a p-i-n-g. Anyway, take my word for it, you will hear the difference. When hitting a top spin shot picture your racquet traveling from a low to high pattern, with the racquet face vertical on contact, parallel to the net. By low I mean dropping the racquet down at least to your knees or below the path of the ball. Then swing up, finishing at least as high as your shoulder.

A good way to practice the proper swing for a top spin shot is to either go to the net or, if you are at home, your garage door, and just practice your brushing action in front of the net or the door. This added practice will help you get the feel required for the shot.

Keep these points in mind while practicing your top spin shots:

1. Your swing is forward and at the same time upward.
2. Bend your knees slightly on the backswing, then on your forward swing lift your body while straightening your legs. This lifting action will give you more power, spin, and control.
3. Your follow-through will be a little higher than normal.
4. For added spin, if you are ready to handle it, gradually shift your grip toward a western grip. I call this slight change of grip a semi-western grip, which is easier to master.
5. For additional spin, tilt your racquet slightly toward the court, closing the racquet face.
6. You will have to swing a little harder due to the brushing action used.

The advantages to using top spin are:

1. Gives you a greater margin for error.
2. You can hit the ball harder and still keep it in the court.
3. Will produce a higher bounce that your opponent will have to adjust to.
4. Can generate slightly more power.

The disadvantages are:

1. It will take more time to develop your timing.
2. You may have to swing slightly harder to get the ball over the net.

41

Underspin

THE OTHER MAIN TYPE of spin is underspin. Underspin is caused by hitting the ball near the bottom, causing reverse spin. It revolves with a counterclockwise motion. This type of motion will cause the ball to stay low throughout its path of flight, especially when it makes contact with the court. Underspin should be used only for mixing your strokes up, for returning high ground strokes, for returning serves, for volleys, so the ball won't float, and for mixing up your approach shots. Too many players try to use underspin on their passing shots, but they keep forgetting they aren't Ken Rosewall, the expert of the underspin shot. Due to the path the underspin shot follows, it is not recommended for passing shots for a lot of players. Even though the ball stays low, your margin for error is too slim.

When hitting an underspin shot keep these fundamentals in mind:

1. Your swing starts from about the height of your shoulder, above the height of the ball. After contact the racquet is lower than the flight of the ball, waist high. In other words, it is a high to low swing.
2. The racquet face is leveled at approximately a forty-five degree angle.

Advantages of using underspin are:

1. It will keep the ball low over the net.
2. If executed correctly, there will be little bounce.
3. Your opponent will have to bend his knees more.

The disadvantages are:

1. Your margin for error is eliminated.
2. If hit too late, the ball will float.

Both types of spin will take a watchful eye, as well as hours of practice to develop them to their potential.

Sidespin

ANOTHER TYPE OF SPIN is sidespin. It is used on your ground strokes to pull an opponent off the court. This will open up the court for your next shot. To execute this type of spin, as you bring your racquet through the hitting zone, turn your racquet strings slightly toward the outside of the court and swing in that direction. Follow through high and to your side. The difficulty of this stroke lies in the fact that you are changing the hitting zone and path of your normal racquet swing. Before attempting this advanced spin in a match, practice it to get the feel for it. First aim your shots down the middle of the court, giving yourself plenty of room for error. Once you get the feel, you can aim a little wider. Jimmy Connors and Chris Evert Lloyd have very effective sidespin shots from anywhere on the court. You can, too, with practice.

Racquet Motion

THERE ARE TWO BASIC stroking motions in tennis today: the straight swing and the looping swing. Both have their advantages and disadvantages. It is up to you to know which one you use, because it will help you in knowing what your stroke looks like, and what you might be doing wrong.

The ready position for the straight swing consists of holding the racquet approximately waist high with racquet and arm relatively straight, pointing toward the net. As you rotate your shoulders, keep your arm relatively straight, but relaxed, and take your racquet straight back so that the tip of your racquet is pointing to the back fence. Your forward swing is from low to high, in a straight path, in the direction in which you want the ball to travel. Your follow-through finishes nice and high.

The straight swing is the simplest of the two types, since there

Straight Backswing

A

A. Assume ready position. B. Pivot so that your side is to the net as you take your racquet back. C. You are prepared for the ball when the "butt" of the racquet is pointing straight ahead.

B

C

Loop Backswing

A

A. Assume a good ready position. B. Pivot and take racquet back. C. Prepare for ball with the "butt" of racquet pointing down toward the court.

B

C

are fewer mechanical aspects that can go wrong. It is the preferred style for beginners.

When using a looping swing, your ready position tends to be slightly higher than that of a straight swing. The racquet is at an angle of approximately forty-five degrees, and your arm is slightly bent. From this position you rotate your shoulders, keeping your racquet up and arm bent, taking your racquet back so that the tip is again pointing to the back fence. Then as the ball approaches you drop the racquet to a position lower than your contact point, or about knee high, straightening your arm with your forward swing going from low to high. Your follow-through should be similar to that of a straight swing, finishing at least shoulder high.

The main differences in the two styles are in your ready position and in your backswing.

If you already have a looping swing, or are deciding to try it, make sure your loop is a compact one. Players have trouble with a looping swing, because the loop gets too big to handle. Your loop, or the tip of your racquet, should only come as high as your shoulder. The looping swing is more difficult because it is harder to time your swing. It is basically just a more complicated stroke, due to the fact that it takes more time to complete.

The advantages of a looping swing, though they are relative, are that you can generate a little more power. It also makes it easier to hit topspin.

The Serve

THE SERVE IS THE MEANS of delivering the ball from behind the baseline by tossing the ball in the air with your hand, and hitting it into your opponent's proper service court before the ball bounces. Though the motion is generally overhead, it is perfectly legal to serve underhand as long as the ball doesn't bounce first. This is the first stroke of each point. The serving motion is similar to throwing a ball overhand. For this reason, girls have a harder time serving than boys because they don't use that motion very often. A good indicator for power on the serve is to see how well you can throw the ball.

This is the only stroke in the game where you are already in perfect position, and your opponent has to wait for you to deliver the ball. Be sure to take your time to prepare for each serve. Don't be in a hurry to start the point. Be prepared mentally as well as physically. At this moment you are in complete control of the point, so it is important you take advantage of it. You do so by either moving your opponent out of position, or by serving in such a manner that your opponent hits a weak return. Know what you are going to do before you serve. The serve is the most important stroke in singles, and the second most important one in doubles. It is more important in singles since you must hold serve to win the match, and you serve every other game. In doubles you serve every fourth game.

Your goals as a server will vary depending upon your ability level. Once you have become proficient at one level, then, and only then, should you move up to the next level. This may take some time, so be patient. Your serving priorities are:

1. Simply get the ball into play.
2. Direction: to improve your game you must be able to serve to the backhand corner.
3. Depth: deep in the service boxes is preferred.
4. Spin: top spin, slice, American Twist.
5. Pace.

When you are just starting out you should only be concerned with serving the ball consistently into the proper service court. By consistently I mean getting 70 percent of your first serves in. Once this has been accomplished then you can concern yourself with direction, moving the ball around in the service court. Serving to a player's backhand is the most difficult of placements, but also the most important. Since most players' weaker return is on their backhand side, you must be able to get the serve there. To win more games I would recommend serving two-thirds of your serves to your opponent's backhand side thus making them hit a weaker return. Depth can be added at, or near, the same time. It is vital to keep the ball deep on your serve, especially the second serve, otherwise your opponent can move in and put you on the defense. The addition of spins to your serves will make your serving more enjoyable and more difficult for your opponent. At the same time it can be a frustrating experience since it is a harder concept to develop. Spin serves can pull your opponent out of position, produce weak returns, and set you up for easy volleys.

Almost any player can serve the ball hard, but what good does it do if you can't find the court? Through my teaching experiences I have seen many players with "cannon ball" serves. Unfortunately

47

Serve

A. Assume a good ready position. B. After your arms have gone down together, raise them simulataneously. C. Release the ball (toss) and lean into the power position. D. Make contact with the ball with your arm extended in front of you. E. Finish the follow-through with the racquet on the opposite side from where it started.

A

B

C

they needed a service court twice the normal size. Serve as hard as you can without sacrificing consistency.

Since the serve is the most complicated stroke in the game, and for that reason the hardest to learn, it is important to break down the parts of the serve by concentrating on one aspect at a time. The parts of the serve are:

1. Stance or positioning
2. Grip
3. Toss
4. Racquet movement

Stance

Where and how you position yourself for the serve has a lot to do with where the serve will go. Your position will vary in singles and doubles and if you are attempting to pull your opponent out of position. In singles, as a rule, you usually stand with your side to the

49

net, so that your front foot is pointing toward the net post, and your back foot is parallel to the baseline. This is contrary to John McEnroe's serving style. Actually, John is the exception. He positions himself as if he is going to serve to the court next to him. This technique forces him to get more of his body into the serve. I would not recommend this style due to the added difficulty. Only John has the patent on it. You should be positioned in such a way that, if you laid your racquet down from the toes of your front foot to the other, your racquet would then be pointing to the middle of the service court. Your feet should be located slightly behind the baseline, and just to the right or left of the service mark, depending on which service court you are aiming for. When first learning to serve it is important *not* to move your feet. The reason most players move their feet on the serve is to chase a poor toss, and once you do that you might as well forget about having a good serve. If you alter your position, your motion has to be changed. When that happens you are more likely to get a poor serve. One way to keep your feet stationary is to imagine they are encased in cement. If you still have trouble, put most of your weight on your front foot or move slightly back from the baseline. As a last resort, place an extra racquet in front of you as you serve and try not to step on it. When you are in ready position to serve you should be relaxed, with your weight slightly forward and your knees slightly bent. You want your weight forward so your toss will be out in front of you, enabling you to get more power in your serve, and at the same time this prepares you for serving and rushing the net, if that is your strategy.

For serving in doubles the same basic fundamentals apply, only your position will be altered. Instead of serving near the center mark, you now move over to approximately halfway between the center mark and singles side line. The purpose of this move is to better position yourself to cover the return of serve, and you won't be so apt to give your partner a sudden pain in the back area. It also makes it easier to serve wide to your opponents' forehands and down the middle of the service box.

Grip

The grip you use when you serve should be like any other grip in that it is comfortable for *you*. The most commonly used and preferred grip is the continental, though the eastern forehand can be used. The advantages of a continental grip are that it makes it easier to snap your wrist, giving you added power. At the same time it makes it easier

Here is a good example of the classic "frying pan" grip in action. Do you use this grip? If so, head back to the kitchen.

for you to apply spin to the ball. No matter what grip you choose it should be a loose one. A loose grip shows that you are relaxed, while enabling you to use your wrist more. Be sure that it is not so loose that you end up serving your racquet as well as the ball. I broke a racquet once that way. This, along with the overhead, are the only strokes where the more wrist action the better the stroke. By "wrist snap" I am referring to the movement of the wrist during the serve. This action is upward in nature. A good way to practice your wrist snap is to practice serving from the service line. From this position it is necessary to have a good "snap" in order to get the ball into the service court.

Your racquet at this time should be pointed toward the proper service court. It should be held at or near waist height, with your tossing hand positioned below the throat of the racquet. The "frypan grip" which is used occasionally should only be used in the kitchen. You can locate this poor excuse for a grip by placing your racquet on the court and picking it up. The "V" and the palm will be on top of the grip. This may be a good grip for flipping pancakes, however, all it can do for your serve is hurt it. This grip causes loss in power potential and makes it literally impossible to put any kind of spin on the ball. If done often enough it can cause tennis elbow.

51

Toss

The toss is the hardest aspect of the serve to master. Toss is a poor definition for the motion involved. When you think of the word toss, what generally comes to your mind is the movement involved when tossing a baseball or football. This is where we get into trouble. Instead of thinking of tossing the ball, picture placing or lifting the ball into position. This motion should be done slowly and smoothly. From your ready positon your tossing or lifting hand should drop slowly down to your front leg, and from there rise slowly until your arm is straight. If you release the ball too early, the toss will be low or it will be too far out in front of you. In either case the result is the same—a bad serve. If you release the ball too late, you will find the ball behind you making it almost physically impossible to snap your wrist. The ball should be released when, and only when, your arm is straight. If you can do this, the ball only needs to rise approximately one-and-a-half feet. So you can see you don't need to toss the ball, just let it float out of your hand, as a balloon would.

A vast number of tennis players have a common problem in their serve—the low toss, which this player is demonstrating for us. It is possible to have a respectable serve even if your toss is low; the result will be a flat serve that barely misses the top of the net. It would be better if you could make contact with the toss where you should. Some players, due to injury, can't reach that high. A higher toss will enable the server to add more pace and spin to the ball. With a lower toss it is almost impossible to add pace or spin.

This player shows what you might look like when you are waiting for your ball toss to come back down so that you can hit it. There is a fine example of a "moon-ball" toss.

It is important, if you are to have a good serve, to know how to hold the ball. You want to cradle the ball between your fingertips and the palm of your hand. If the ball is either too far out on the fingertips or held in the palm of your hand, the ball will come out spinning. Serving a ball that is spinning is much harder to control than one with no rotation. You can either hold the ball as if you were holding a glass of water or, the way I prefer, with the palm up. Also it is wise to hold just one ball at a time when serving. The only thing the other ball does is get in the way, unless, of course, you always miss your first serve. It is uncomfortable running all over the court carrying a ball in your hand. If you drop it or place it on the court, you will probably end up tripping over it. If you use a two-handed backhand, then you are really in a predicament. So find some place within your clothing to hold the second ball.

Before you release the ball you should already know where the ball will stop. The place where the ball stops, besides being known as your contact point, is also described as your target zone. You should be able to imagine a target in the air approximately one-and-a-half feet above your outstretched arm, or as high as you can reach with your racquet. Your target is also located about one-and-a-half feet in front of your lead foot. If you can't imagine this then just humor me. You must be able to hit this target with your ball release every time if you are to have a consistent serve. If you can't consistently hit your target, then you need to practice, yes, I said practice, your toss. Unfortunately, not enough players do this. You will be amazed what just a little practice of your tossing action will do for your serve.

You can practice your toss by using three different approaches. First, you can simply hold your racquet up at your contact point and toss the ball up to your strings. Or you can place your racquet on the court about a foot and a half in front of your lead foot. Then gently toss the ball up and make it land on your racquet face. The only drawback with this technique is that a good toss means you are rewarded by chasing the ball all over the court after it bounces off your racquet. Finally, you can go back to one of the fences surrounding the court and practice lifting the ball up so it follows one of the poles. Here again, it should only be tossed as high as you can reach.

Hitting a serve blindfolded is not as difficult as it looks. Almost anyone, given a sufficient amount of practice, can do it. The keys to hitting it consistently are knowing where your toss will be and keeping your head up.

Serving from behind a rebound net is one of the best ways to improve your serve. It forces you to reach up for the ball while putting some spin on it. For additional practice for putting top spin on your serves, try serving from your knees or while lying on your back.

No matter how high you toss a ball in the air, there is a moment at its apex when the ball stops completely before it starts to descend. This is when you want to make contact with the ball. It is much easier to hit a ball that is completely stopped than one that is moving. If you watch the ball carefully you can see if you are hitting your serve while the ball is still moving, and, if so, you need some more practice.

Racquet movement

You will find that your racquet movement can be easy if you do it slowly and remember "down-together up-together." Watch Jimmy Connors sometime and see how slow his motion is until he gets into the "power" position. From your ready position your racquet slowly drops straight down so that the tip of it is pointing to the court. At the same time your tossing arm goes down. Then, as your tossing arm goes up, so does your racquet. It is your objective here to keep both arms moving simultaneously and in the same basic direction. As your racquet travels upward, still in slow motion, it should get to a point where your racquet tip is pointing to the back fence. If you use your imagination while in this position you can picture yourself forming the letter "Y." From here, since your grip is relaxed, the racquet should automatically drop down to the "power position." This position has also been referred to as the "back-scratch" and "hammer-nail" positions. No matter what your terminology, this position is the source of your power. Some very well-known players started out serving from this position. This is an excellent position for beginners to learn. The racquet motion up to this point will give you 10 percent more power, give you your needed rhythm, and make you look like you know what you're doing. In the power position your elbow should be slightly lower than your shoulder. Then from this position your racquet movement speeds up and you rotate your shoulders, so that when you make contact with the ball, the racquet is traveling as fast as possible. The movement from the power position until you make contact with the ball is upward and forward in nature. Here you want to emphasize reaching *up* for the ball. If you are not reaching up, then you are pushing the ball. This will only harm your serve.

Some experts of the game like to speak of "pronation" of the racquet. In layman's terms this means to turn your wrist inward or outward. This will give you the spin, power, and direction you need. This motion will allow you to hit better serves down the middle and to the backhand corner. Then, after you make contact with the ball, it is vital that you have a good follow-through. Players who are not relaxed enough will have a very slight follow-through. Your follow-through should finish with your racquet on the opposite side of your body. One way to judge your serving ability is to serve blindfolded or with your eyes closed. If your serve is smooth and your toss where it should be, even if you are a beginner, you shouldn't have any trouble hitting the ball.

As in any other stroke, spin is very important to your serving game. Being able to move the ball around with spin will give an added dimension to your game.

There are two basic types of spin used when serving. One is top spin that, even if you aren't aware of it, is always on the ball, and slice. The American twist is also used, but has declined in popularity due to difficulty in mastering it. To make the spin serve easy, keep this basic concept in mind: the main difference in spins serves and the so-called flat serve is how the racquet travels at the point of contact.

Anytime you reach up for the ball on the serve and hit it at its apex, you are hitting with some top spin. You should be able to hear the difference when you hit with spin and when you don't. You will

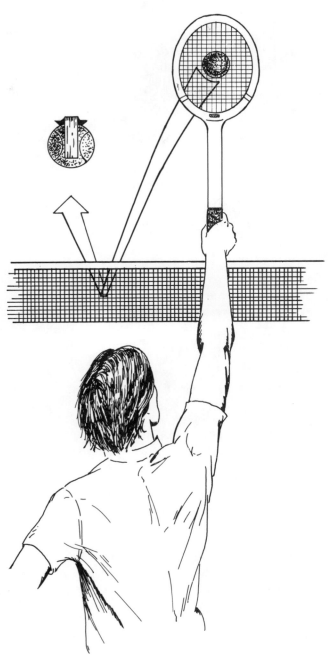

Top Spin Serve

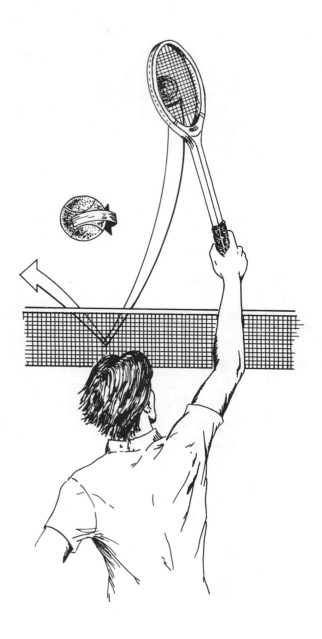

Slice Serve

hear a kind of "pinging" sound the same as with the ground strokes. For added top spin concentrate on brushing the face of your racquet up the backside of the ball in the same manner as you would with a top spin ground stroke. As you make contact with the ball your racquet face should be parallel to the net. Two good ways to develop an effective top spin serve are to practice serving over a rebound net or over a fence surrounding the court.

The other main type of spin used when serving is slice. A slice serve is employed to pull your opponent out of position. It will force him to either hit a weak return or go for a winner. This is a good tactic to use when you serve and rush. A slice serve will open up the court for your first volley.

The slice serve is the easiest of the spin serves to develop. Before you attempt hitting a slice serve, practice bouncing a ball and hitting it on the side of the frame. Then practice the same technique, this time hitting the ball with the strings on the outside of the ball. Doing this will develop the necessary feel for the stroke, and at the same time you will hear the pinging sound.

Now when you step up to the baseline, humor me again. Hit your first few practice serves using the frame of your racquet, just as you did when you bounced the ball. Even though your balls may land three courts away, you are still learning the required skills necessary for an effective slice serve. (To learn this serve easier, start out at first with the racquet already in the power position.) After you have chased down your balls, practice hitting a slice serve by making contact with the outside of the ball, just as you did when you bounced the balls. As you make contact with the ball your racquet face will be perpendicular to the net, and you will use a slight cupping action coming around the ball. In doing this you will hit just a very small section of the ball, as if you were slicing off a part of the ball. This is how "slice serve" got its name. Your follow-through will be just like your top spin serve with the racquet finishing on the opposite side of the body.

A third type of serve, which I don't recommend using unless you feel that it is absolutely necessary, is the American twist serve. This serve should only be attempted by advanced players, since it is so difficult to learn and physically demanding. The advantage of this serve is that once it hits the court it bounces high and to your opponent's backhand if you are right-handed. This is one of the most difficult shots to return.

In order to hit an effective American twist serve, it is necessary to change your ball toss. This is another reason for the difficulty with

American Twist Serve

this serve, you are now required to learn to toss the ball to another target zone. Having one target to aim for is hard enough, let alone two. Your placement or toss now needs to be about a foot to your left and a foot behind if you are right-handed. This means you have to arch your back more with this type of serve. Be sure to stretch your back muscles before attempting this serve. It is easy to strain some muscles due to the over-stretching of the back necessary for this serve.

As you make contact with the ball your racquet face travels from left to right and parallel to the net. Your follow-through on this serve finishes with the racquet on the same side of the body from which it started.

Except for the American twist serve, your ball toss should not be altered for different serves. Once you start doing that you lose your consistency. Also, if you change ball placements, you are going to have to practice all these different tosses. A good returner will be able to notice if you alter your ball toss and be able to adjust for it before you serve, thus you will lose the serve's effectiveness. Don't give your spin serve away by signaling ahead to the returner by using various ball tosses.

Serve and Rush

A GOOD STRATEGY, in singles or doubles, is serving and rushing the net. However, if your volleys need some work, you might want to save this tactic until they improve. Or you might take the opposite approach and make yourself serve and rush so you are forced to hit your volleys.

Before you step up to the baseline to serve, you should already have decided if you are going to use this tactic. If you wait until you admire your serve it will be too late. By that time you are just inside the baseline and the ball will be at your feet, and you know what that means—trouble. Once you have made up your mind that you are going to rush the net, nothing should stop you, not even a weak serve. By that time it will be too late to change your mind.

Immediately after you hear contact made, then and not before, is the time to start to the net. If you start any earlier you will be looking down too early and the ball will go into the net. Remember this tactic is called "serve and rush," not serve and take your time up to the net. Many players take their time and then they wonder why they weren't in position for their first volley. Unless you are a top quality tournament player, you won't get up to your ready position at the net for your first volley. Don't worry about it. It really doesn't matter how far you get as long as you get as far as you physically can and do your split-step. If you remember nothing else, remember to do your necessary split-step. The split-step slows down your momentum for a split second until you have time to determine in which direction to move for your volley. Your split-step must be done just before your opponent makes contact with his service return. Any sooner, and you won't get up to the net before next Friday; any later, and you'll be watching the ball whiz by for a winner.

Serve and Rush

A. Assume a good ready position. This is the moment when you decide you are going to serve and rush. B. After your arms have gone down, raise them simultaneously. C. Release the ball (toss) and lean into the power position. This time the toss may be slightly out in front of you. D. Make contact with the ball with your arm extended out in front of you. E. Instead of leaving your feet in place, step into the court and start to rush the net. F. Continue to rush the net. G. Prepare for a split-step. H. This is the split-step position. I. If you see that a forehand volley is coming, this is how you should move to the ball with your raquet prepared. J. Make contact with the ball well out in front of you. K. This is the proper follow-through.

A
B

C

D

E

F

G

H

I

J

K

Now you are ready for your first volley. Your first volley is usually not a put-away volley. It is very hard to hit a winning volley from behind the service line which is probably where you will be. Your first volley should be hit deep into the court moving your opponent around, and allowing you time to make it up to your homebase. There is where you want to be in order to hit your winning volley. You will be closer to the net where you can hit down on the ball, and where you have a greater variety of angles to choose from.

Practice your serve

The serve is the only stroke you can truly practice by yourself. So, when you can't find anyone to play or practice with, take some balls out and practice your serves, even your second serve. For excitement make some targets to aim for. You can either use tennis ball cans or four balls stacked in the shape of a pyramid. To test the pace on your serves, see how many bounces it takes for your ball to get to the back fence after it has first landed in the proper service box. The fewer the bounces, the more powerful the serve. You should only practice on the average for ten to fifteen minutes, otherwise your arm will get sore, and you will lose interest. Make your practice fun, and improve your serve. For players just starting out, and even for those of us who are veterans, refining our serves can be one of the hardest things we ever do.

Before you attempt a serve, I would recommend just throwing some balls overhand. You will find this motion very similar to your service motion. This is also a good way to loosen up the muscles needed for your serve. Another way to loosen up those muscles is to take an old racquet out into the yard and throw it as you go through your service motion. This will emphasize throwing your racquet at the ball. That's just what you want to do on your serve, except for letting go of the racquet.

Next I would suggest practicing your ball toss, using one or more of the techniques already mentioned. Since this is the single most difficult aspect of the *game* to master, it should be practiced daily.

Instead of serving using the full motion, begin by starting with your racquet already in the "power position." From here just simply toss the ball and meet it with the racquet in the proper spot. At this point don't be concerned with getting the ball over the net or the follow-through.

After you can do all that consistently, aim for the proper service box and finish with a good follow-through. It's hard to say how long it will take you to master this motion. Don't be concerned, just take your time, and wait until you get it right.

The next step is to start out in your ready position, with your racquet and body pointing to the proper service court. Simultaneously drop both arms, leaving your tossing arm down until you have completed your motion with your racquet to get it into the power position. Then gently toss the ball and hit it just hard enough to get it into the proper service court. When you are ready, you can put the full motion together. Following these procedures is bound to help your serve and your game. Be sure to practice each part of the serve before moving on to the next step.

The most asked questions about the serve

1. What causes my serve to go into the net?
Answer: This is the most common error dealing with the serve, so don't feel alone. There are many reasons for your problem: Looking down too early, which takes your eyes off the ball. Trying to hit a so-called flat serve. Pulling your shoulder down too soon. Your ball toss is too low. Your ball toss is too far out in front of you. You're trying to put too much spin on the ball. You're trying to serve and rush before you have made contact with the ball. Lack of follow-through.

2. What causes my serve to go long?
Answer: Either your ball toss is too high, which makes it hard to judge the ball; your ball toss is behind you, making it impossible to snap your wrist, and your racquet face is open on impact; or you are pushing the ball, in which case the toss isn't high enough to enable you to snap your wrist. You also might be using the "frying pan" grip.

3. What can I do to lower my ball toss?
Answer: A high ball toss can be better described by such terms as a "jack-in-the-box" toss or a "moon-ball" toss. In other words, this is the toss where you can go and get a drink and still get back in time to hit the serve. If you have this problem I offer three suggestions: practice your toss, slow the motion of your toss up, and make sure your serving motion is continuous. If you have a hitch or pause in your motion it is usually a result of having a high ball toss.

4. How can I cure my "lasso" motion?
Answer: In most cases you are not even aware this is occurring, unless someone tells you. The lasso motion happens when you bring your

racquet up and make a small loop with your racquet before starting your upward movement. To remedy this problem, make sure your toss isn't too high. If you have the proper ball toss and a continuous serving motion this problem cannot occur.

5. How can I stop foot faulting?
Answer: A foot fault occurs when you step on the baseline or inside the court before you make contact on the serve. First of all foot faulting is illegal by the tennis rules, so should not be permitted. However, if you find yourself doing it, you can prevent foot faulting by keeping the majority of your body weight on your lead foot; having a proper ball toss; moving back a few inches from the baseline; and avoiding using a rocking action during your serve. During practice, place something in front of the baseline so if you move your foot you will hit the object and be aware of the foot fault. You foot fault for one of three reasons: you are unaware that you are doing it, in which case you should be made aware of your mistake by a friend or your local pro; you are too lazy to care; or you are doing it for an advantage. The advantages of foot faulting are slightly more power behind the serve and the chance to get to the net faster.

When you find an opponent foot faulting, you should first keep your cool. He may or may not be doing it intentionally, so ask him if he is aware of what he is doing. In that case he will usually try to correct it. However, if he is aware of it and makes no effort to stop, you have a decision to make. If it is just a friendly match, you can either forget about it and concentrate on your service return or walk off the court. There is no reason you have to play with someone who cheats, and that is exactly what he is doing. If this happens in a tournament, call a foot fault. This is hard to do in singles, since you should be watching the ball and not the server's feet. Sometimes in the warm-up you can discover this. It is easier to call in doubles by the player not returning serve. In fact, that is one of his responsibilities. In either case, if you call a foot fault and your opponent gets upset, which he probably will, he has a choice to make: either to stop foot faulting or call for a lines judge. If you do call for a judge, remember if he calls foot faults for one person, he has to call them for everyone. That is the rule. So make sure you don't foot fault or calling for a lines judge might just backfire.

6. I've been told that my ball toss is too low. What can I do about it?
Answer: Raise it! Now wasn't that easy? Actually, as you know, altering or changing your toss is one of the hardest aspects of the game.

When you make your ball toss, make sure that your arm is fully extended before you let go of the ball. In most cases that is the leading cause for a low toss. Then just practice your toss daily using the three methods already mentioned.

Return of Serve

THE SERVICE RETURN IS the most important shot in doubles, and second in importance only to the serve in singles. It is more important in doubles, since you return serve twice as often as you serve. As always, consistency is the main objective with this, as with any other shot. If you are going to break your opponent's serve you must get a high percentage of the returns back into play, no matter what it takes.

If you win the toss or spin of the racquet and you have a good consistent service return, a good strategy would be to elect to return serve, hoping to get an early service break and put added pressure on your opponent. If your game plan calls for percentage tennis, which it should, then going for outright winners on the return are a no-no. The odds for hitting an outright winner on the service return are slim at best, so wait for a better opportunity to hit your winner. Any type of winner from the baseline, no matter if it is a ground stroke, return or serve, or overhead, are low percentage shots and only should be used as a last resort. Your homebase at the net is where most of your winners should occur. Remember the server has the advantage, he or she should know where the serve is going and you don't, so play it safe.

The server must wait for you, the returner, to be ready before he serves. So, as with the serve, prepare yourself both mentally and physically. If he serves when you are not ready, do not attempt to return it. A let must be called when this happens. If you attempt to return the serve, even though you are not ready, the point must stand.

When returning serve three options are open to you:

1. Down-the line
2. Crosscourt
3. Lob

The down-the-line return must be used most sparingly to keep your opponent honest. It is good to make some so that he will have to guard against the shot.

The crosscourt return of serve is the easiest. The net is lowest at that point, there is more court to hit into, and any ball is easier to return if it is returned in the same direction from which it came. When returning crosscourt or down-the-line against a net rusher in either singles or doubles, aim your returns for the service line. This will force your opponent into hitting a low volley or half volley. In either case, it is a difficult shot and will put the server on the defense.

The lob return of serve is a good tactic for mixing up your game. It can be especially effective against a net rusher. This type of return will work more effectively for you near the end of a match when your opponent is more tired.

Against an opponent who serves and stays back, you should usually hit a crosscourt return and make the ball land between the service line and the baseline.

Spin of either type should be put on your returns. If the serve bounces high, underspin is recommended for control; otherwise top spin should be used to return most serves. As you know, top spin will give you the greatest margin for error. The type of return style you employ will depend upon these three key ingredients:

1. Your ability to return serve.
2. The type of court surface.
3. The server's ability.

Your ability will dictate whether you stay back after you return, or if you rush the net. The type of court surface will also play a part in your return of serve. If the surface is slow, such as clay, you have more time to prepare for the return. Your swing and strategy may be altered. However, the main determining factor on the type of return you use is the server's ability. If the server uses a lot of spin, then you will have to alter where you position yourself in your ready position. Depending on the type of spin used, you may want to move a couple of steps either to the left or right, while also moving a couple of steps forward. Your moving ready position has been altered so that you can cut off the angle of the serve. In the case of excessive top spin or American twist get to the ball quickly before it has had time to bounce over your head. If your opponent has a hard, fast serve, it would be wise to move your ready position back a few feet to give you more time to pick up the ball and react to it. Bjorn Borg has one of the best returns of serve in the game. He stands farther back than any other pro, usually eight to ten feet behind the baseline. However when he meets the ball he is moving foreward and ends up only a few feet behind the baseline. If your opponent has a weak serve, you have one of two options. You can take a little bit bigger backswing and put more pace on the return to try to force your opponent into an error. Or you can move inside your baseline, and after you hit the return, move into the net.

Return of Serve

A. The ready position. B. Beginning the turn and starting to take the racquet back. C. Racquet back in the abbreviated position, ready to hit the return. D. Just before contact with the ball. E. Follow-through.

A   B

C

D

E

Your normal position when returning serve is two to three feet behind the baseline. In this position you could draw a straight line from the server to you and the line would bisect the court into two equal parts. If you have a tendency to favor one side over the other, your opponent should be able to see it and take advantage of it.

As the ball is tossed you need to "unwait." Bounce up and down to get the lead out of your feet so you can react more quickly. The serve is the hardest type of ball to watch. The reason is that it comes off your opponent's racquet so quickly. You need to concentrate totally on the ball from the moment the server begins his motion until after you hear your racquet make contact with the ball. If you are like me and have some trouble watching the ball on the return, use the bounce-hit technique that insures greater concentration. If you are watching the toss carefully you should be able to see if your opponent tosses the ball in a different spot depending upon the type of serve used, though the server should not be doing it. However, if they do, you will know what type of serve will be coming and you can prepare early for it.

As soon as you can distinguish whether it will be a forehand or backhand return, rotate your shoulders, taking your racquet to the modified position. It is important that you think of the return of serve as just what it is, and not a typical ground stroke, otherwise you will be using too big a backswing in most cases. This modified position requires taking the racquet two-thirds of the way back or less. Your main goal is to just get the ball back into play, and, since the necessary power is already on the ball, this is all the backswing you really need. Remember the ball is coming at you twice as fast as a normal ground stroke so you won't have your normal time to prepare. From the modified backswing position, at the proper time, get at least one good step forward, meeting the ball out in front of the body at the normal contact point. It is important to be sure to hit through the ball on the return. Otherwise the return is likely to go into the net due to the shortened backswing. Your follow-through should be your normal elongated and high one.

If you decide to employ the tactic of returning the serve and rushing the net, make the decision before the server serves. Otherwise, if you wait to see what type of serve is used or wait to admire your return, you won't have enough time to get to your homebase at the net. If you wait this long, you will find yourself hitting too many of those dreaded half volleys. When that happens your tactic has back-fired.

Return of Serve and Rush

A. Assume the ready position. B. Move in to hit the return on the rise. C. Stop the momentum just long enough to prepare to hit the return of serve. D. Hit the return of serve. E. Follow through while beginning to rush to the net. F. Continue to rush the net. G. Take a split-step. H. Hit a winning volley. I. Follow-through.

A

B

C

D

E

F

G

H

I

On the second serve you might like to take a chance and alter your position slightly so that you can "run around" your backhand and hit a forehand return. In most cases this should be done as your opponent is tossing the ball, otherwise he will have time to change his serve.

It is best to return serve and rush on a weak serve, that is, if your opponent usually has a weak serve, or on the second serve that is generally easier to handle. As the server tosses the ball, when he is concentrating on the toss, sneak inside the baseline as far as you can get. Then just before contact is made, do your famous "split-step." This will halt your momentum just long enough to get yourself under control and get you into position to make a good return. After you have made solid contact with the ball, continue up to your home-base at the net. This type of return is not used to hit a winner, but rather to put added pressure on the server and get you into a position where you can hit a winner. It should be hit to your opponent's backhand, since that is usually his weakest stroke. Another tactic you can employ is to move inside the baseline a few feet before the server prepares himself. This will make the server think twice before he serves and will put added pressure on him. Be sure to use this tactic on the second serve only.

Returning keys to keep in mind:

1. Make sure you are in the proper position to return the serve.
2. Try to anticipate the type of serve placement so you can be better prepared.
3. Get the ball back any way you can. A must, if you are to have any chance at winning the point.
4. Hit a good enough return to put the server on the defense.
5. When the opportunity presents itself, get to the net as soon as possible.

The most asked questions about the return of serve

1. What causes me to mis-hit my returns?
Answer: When you mis-hit your return of serve it is usually for one or more of these reasons: you are positioning yourself too close for the speed of the serve, your backswing is too big for the same reason, you are not in a good ready position, or you are not watching the ball close enough.

76

2. Where should I aim my returns?

Answer: The same options are open to you in both singles and doubles. Though in doubles, you must remember there is a net person ready to put the ball away. If your ability allows, you should mix up your service returns. The safest way to return serve is crosscourt, because it is always easier to return a ball in the same direction from which it came, the net is lower in the middle, and you have more court to aim for. Against a net rusher always try to keep the ball relatively close to the net.

3. Should I lob my returns?

Answer: Yes, it is a very good tactic to use, especially in doubles when the server likes to serve and rush. If you don't have a very effective lob, wait until you have more confidence in it.

4. Why do I have more trouble returning serve in doubles than singles?

Answer: The primary reason for this problem is that you are thinking more about your opponent at the net than concentrating on watching the ball. If you look up to see what the net person is doing, how do you expect to be able to watch the ball? So put the net person out of your mind, which I know is impossible for some of you, and just worry about getting the ball back into play. You also have less court to hit into and you must be aware of the angles of the game.

5. How can I get more power into my returns?

Answer: After you can consistently return serve then, and only then, think about adding more power. Remember your main goal is just to get the ball back into play. If more power is required, make sure you (a) hit the ball on the sweet spot (b) get a good step forward into the ball (c) hit through the ball and have a long follow-through.

6. Why do I miss so many of my returns when I am attempting to return and rush?

Answer: Usually because you are thinking of two things at once, returning the serve and getting to the net. Your first objective is to return the serve. After you have done that successfully you can concentrate on getting to the net.

Ground Strokes

GROUND STROKES ARE STROKES you hit near the baseline after the ball has bounced. Most players hit more gound strokes than any other stroke in the game. This statistic will vary depending on your ability level. Your basic objectives with your ground strokes are to:

1. Move your opponent around.
2. Keep the ball deep.
3. Keep the ball in play while making few errors.

Forehand

THE FOREHAND HAS BEEN REFERRED to in terms such as the foundation stroke and the cornerstone of the ground strokes. It is usually hit more often than the backhand and you can usually do more with it. This is generally the first stroke learned. Maybe that is why it is the stroke preferred by most players. By definition the forehand is a ground stroke hit on the right-hand side of the body if you are right-handed, and left if you are left-handed. The forehands tend to be easier for most players since they are used to doing things on that side of their body. You should think of the forehand stroke as an extension of the forearm. If you have trouble executing a forehand, try to imagine hitting the ball with the palm of your hand. Have a friend toss you some balls and gently hit them with the palm of your hand. This will help you to get the feel for the stroke.

A common question arises when hitting a forehand. "What do I do with my opposite hand?" Two answers to this dilemma are: use your opposite hand to point at the ball or just hold it off to the side for better balance. If your arm gets too close to your body there is a tendency to either get too close to the ball or to alter the path of racquet movement by swinging across the hitting zone.

Forehand

A. Assume a good ready position. B. Pivot and take your racquet back. C. With racquet back, you are prepared for the ball. D. Step into the ball making contact with it when it is even with your front foot. E. Finish your follow-through while keeping your eyes focused on the contact point.

A

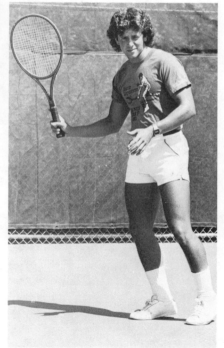

B

C

D

E

While in your moving ready position behind the baseline, make sure your racquet is in a position compatible with your type of swing and that your grip is loose. When you see the ball approaching quickly change grips, if necessary, while at the same time rotate your shoulders and take the racquet back into position, keeping your knees slightly bent. Tighten your grip slightly, remembering that your goal for both ground strokes is to get the racquet back into position before the ball crosses the net.

In both your forehand and backhand, your legs are very important to the outcome of your stroke. As you know, in your ready position your legs should be slightly bent; as you pivot or turn and take your racquet back they should remain the same. As you step forward to make contact with the ball, slightly bend the knees some more as if you were going to sit down in a chair. As you bring your racquet through the hitting zone, straighten your legs. This will give you the additional power and top spin you desire. When you step forward with your left foot and bring your racquet forward to meet the ball, be sure to keep your wrist and grip nice and firm. If you are right-handed, your contact point should be even with your left foot. Your step should be of comfortable length. Finally, as you hit through the ball, your follow-through should finish with the racquet above your head and the racquet face slightly open. When you finish your follow-through, your head should still be down, fixed on your contact point so that your chin is resting on your shoulder. This high follow-through is commonly referred to as "airing the armpit." One main problem with most players' follow-through is that they feel they are required to point the tip of the racquet toward the ball. The two problems that arise here are (a) the ball won't stay on the strings as long, and (b) you will be moving the racquet across the hitting zone instead of through it. When either one of these things occur you lose control of the ball.

Two-Handed Forehand

A FEW PLAYERS USE a two-handed forehand. Maybe some of you are interested in trying it, so I feel this unique ground stroke is worthy of mention. It has been around, at least on the pro circuit, since the days when Pancho Segura used it masterfully. As with the two-handed backhand, this stroke will give you more power and control, but it

81

Two-Handed Forehand

A. Preparing early by taking the racquet back before the ball crosses the net. B.The racquet is back in position soon enough to give the player time to rest for a second. C. About to make contact with the ball when it's even with her front foot. D. After hitting the ball. This is the beginning of the follow-through. Her eyes are still focused on the contact point. E.This much follow-through is not recommended, but in some cases it doesn't hurt.

A

B

C

D

E

will also limit your reach and it is hard to get used to. Your stroking technique is the same as for any other forehand ground stroke. The main decision you have to make in dealing with a two-handed forehand is which grip to use. This will not present a problem if you use the conventional one-handed backhand. If you have a one-handed backhand, your grip should be with your right hand. Your left hand grips below your right. This is similar to a golf or baseball grip with both hands using forehand grips.

If you use a two-handed backhand then you have a choice to make. You can either keep your hands the way they are and juggle your racquet to form the conventional two-handed backhand grip, or hit your two-handed backhand with your hands crossed. Or you can reverse your two-handed forehand grip and keep your normal two-handed backhand grip. The decisions are yours if you choose to try the stroke.

Backhand

THE BACKHAND IS THE ground stroke you hit on the side opposite your dominant hand. If you are right-handed then your backhand will be on your left side.

Contrary to popular belief the backhand ground stroke is a more natural stroke than your forehand. By more natural I am referring to the fact that your hitting arm and shoulder are in front of the body causing freer body movement. I see too many players either running around their backhand to hit a forehand, or moving out of position so they won't have to hit as many backhands. The only things this accomplishes is to make your weak backhand weaker and possibly put you out of position for the next shot.

To improve this, the least favorite stroke in the game, practice it as often as possible. Everyone enjoys practicing shots they are good at, but it takes a willingness to improve one's game to practice one's weaker strokes.

When executing a backhand it may help to imagine hitting the ball with the back part of the hand. This is where they got the name "backhand." Another suggestion, when you are stroking your backhand, is to picture yourself throwing a frisbee but without the wrist action that sometimes occurs.

Inverted Backhand

The disadvantage of using this stroke is that you lack power. It is almost impossible to hit a top spin. Also the bad arm position can cause wrist, forearm, and shoulder problems.

The same basic stroking fundamentals apply to the backhand as to the forehand. Your moving ready position is positioned at your homebase and your grip is nice and loose. When you determine that the ball is coming to your backhand side, rotate your shoulders and take your racquet back. Again your backswing will differ depending on your type of swing. As you are taking your racquet back into position, you should change your grip, if necessary, to the eastern backhand grip. Using this grip will give you a more solid stroke because more of your hand is behind the racquet, giving you greater support. If you use a straight swing, a good reference point to keep in mind is to place your hand on your hip, or anywhere between your waist and knee, on your backswing. This will keep your elbow close to your body and your arm straight. This is important no matter what type of swing you use. It will also keep the racquet low on the backswing.

If you are right-handed, you step into the ball with your right foot. This will give you the momentum and extra power you need.

Your contact point differs from that of your forehand, which is one of the difficulties of the stroke. You need to make contact with the ball at least a foot out in front of your lead foot, as compared to even with your lead foot on your forehand. This split second difference in timing causes many players to misjudge the ball, and, as a result, causes weak backhands. As with the forehand, you hit through the ball, finishing with a nice, high follow-through. Again, remember: *don't* point the racquet tip toward the ball.

If you keep these points in mind and give your backhand its needed practice, there is no reason your backhand can't become your best stroke.

Backhand

A. Assume ready position. B. Pivot and take racquet back. C. Shoulder and butt of racquet should face net while you wait for the ball. D. Make contact with the ball when it is out in front of your front foot. E. Complete the follow-through while still concentrating on the point of contact.

A

B

C

D

E

Two-Handed Backhand

A RELATIVELY NEW and very popular method of hitting a backhand is the two-handed or two-fisted approach. This two-handed backhand has changed the game practically overnight, thanks to the success that Chris Evert Lloyd, Jimmy Connors, and Bjorn Borg have had with it. They certainly make it look easy. Now, children beginning to play earlier and physically weaker players have stronger backhands, thanks to this ingenious approach. Young players and adults alike benefit from the added strength they get by using two hands.

If you are an adult player, set in your ways, it will be hard for you to change to a two-handed backhand. I know because I have tried. But, if you feel this stroke might be for you, be sure to give it enough time to see if it will work. In most cases, depending on how often you play, a month is usually long enough. By then you should know if you are willing to change and if it will help your game. Until then you will have a good excuse if you happen to lose. Also, if you are having any elbow problems, the two-handed backhand just might be the answer. It will take most of the strain from the elbow.

The first question with the two-handed backhand is which grip to use. You have a choice between two regular eastern forehand grips, with your dominant hand at the base. With this grip style you won't have to worry about changing grips. The other style, and most popular, involves using an eastern backhand grip with your dominant hand and an eastern forehand with the other. Obviously, this involves changing grips, though it will give you added support.

Your stroking mechanics will be basically the same as any ground stroke. Either style of swing can be used, although I recommend the straight swing approach.

If you are right-handed, the main point to keep in mind while hitting a two-handed backhand is that your *left* arm is now the dominant one. You should swing as if you were hitting a left-handed forehand. Your right hand is just on there for the added strength factor. A good method in learning a two-handed backhand is to go out with someone on the practice court and hit some left-handed forehands. Besides giving you added strength in your left hand and arm, it will also give you added confidence.

87

Your point of contact will be even with your lead foot. You have three choices on the type of follow-through to use. You can follow through holding the racquet with both hands, finishing as you would with one hand. Or, after you make contact with the ball, you can drop your weaker arm the way Bjorn Borg does. The third method is to finish with the racquet wrapped over your shoulder. This has commonly been referred to as the "strangling" approach. I would not recommend this method for the simple reason that it is unnecessary and a waste of energy.

The advantage to a two-handed backhand is that it gives you added power and control. The only disadvantage is that you have less reach, which means you must have better footwork. If you want to give this method a try and see what it can do for your game, it can't hurt. I have known players to change to a two-handed backhand for a while. When they've gone back to their regular backhand, they've seen some improvement.

Two-Handed Backhand

A. Assume a good ready position. B. Take the raquet back. C. Be prepared for the ball even if it is not yet on your side of the net. D. Step forward into the ball, making contact with it when it is even with your front foot. E. Finish with a nice, high follow-through.

A   B

88

C

D

E

The most asked questions about ground strokes

1. Why do my ground strokes always hit the net?
Answer: It could be for a number of reasons. You are not using any top spin; you look up too early; or you lack follow-through.

2. Why do my ground strokes always go long?
Answer: You are either hitting the ball late; hitting the ball too hard without the necessary spin; or your racquet face is open at point of contact.

3. How can I get more power on my strokes?
Answer: Make sure you hit through the ball using the proper grip. Hit the ball on the sweet spot. Meet the ball out in front of you. Use a loop swing. Rotate your shoulders more and take a little longer swing. This will get more of your body into the stroke. With the backhand, when you lengthen your swing, your back will be turned to the net. Also, be sure to use your legs. The muscles in your legs are stronger than your arms.

4. Why do I always hit the ball late?
Answer: It could be that your racquet doesn't get back into position early enough; your timing is off; or you are not concentrating well enough on the ball.

5. How do you hit the ball crosscourt?
Answer: Make sure you hit the ball out in front of you. As you make contact, your racquet should be pointing crosscourt. Your follow-through should go in the direction you want the ball to go, and you need to hit the outside of the ball.

6. Why am I off balance on my shots?
Answer: You may have poor footwork, and you are either hitting the ball too late or too early. Or your timing is off. The only cure for that is to hit a lot of balls.

7. How can I watch the ball better?
Answer: Use the bounce-hit technique. Don't look up until you *hear* contact with the ball. On your forehand side, keep your head down

until your shoulder touches your chin. Look for the printing on the ball. Always think that the ball you're hitting is the last one you will hit, so make it your best.

8. How can I stop leading with my elbow on my back hand?
Answer: You can push down with your hand so that your arm is straight, but relaxed. Make sure that you lead with your hand. Use a straight backswing, hold your elbow with your other hand. Try a two-handed backhand, or use the famous ball-under-your-armpit technique.

9. How can I avoid using too much wrist?
Answer: Make sure your wrist and arm are firm throughout the stroke. Be sure to hit through the ball. Lengthen your follow-through in the direction you want the ball to go. Do not point the tip of the racquet toward the ball at the end of your follow-through. Be sure you are holding your racquet above the butt of the racquet, well up on the grip.

10. How can I lengthen my follow-through?
Answer: After each stroke check your follow-through. If it is too short, fake your follow-through and finish it where it should be. After doing that enough times your long follow-through will come naturally. Remember on each follow-through to finish with the racquet at least head high, and "air the armpit." You also might try to catch your racquet at the end of your follow-through.

11. I am a right-handed player and my left hand crosses over my body. What can I do?

Answer: When this happens you are generally too close to the ball. Make sure your footwork is correct and that you are in the proper position to hit the stroke. Bringing your left hand across the body will also throw your balance off. The best way I know to prevent this from happening is to point your left hand at the ball until just before contact, and to catch your racquet with your left hand on your follow-through.

12. How can I get my racquet back more quickly?
Answer: This means you are not reacting to the ball quickly enough. Make your goal to get your racquet into position *before* the ball crosses the net. Be sure to be on the balls of your feet so that you can react

faster. Also try to watch the ball come off your opponent's racquet. Practice some mirror tennis to work on getting the racquet back fast. Have someone call out "forehand" or "backhand" for you and see how long it takes for you to get ready.

High Ground Strokes

HIGH GROUND STROKES are ground strokes you hit when the ball is near shoulder height, anywhere on the court. So don't think of them as regular ground strokes, because they aren't. The reason most players panic when one comes is because they just don't know what to do, and they don't see them often enough. What you need do, then, is to practice them.

There are three basic techniques involved in hitting high ground strokes. Which one you use is determined by your ability and the ability of your opponent.

To tell if you will have to hit a high ground stroke, you must watch the flight of the ball. If the ball travels more than three feet above the net, you should know that the ball will bounce relatively high. If your opponent puts excessive top spin on the ball it will bounce even higher. So be ready.

The easiest way, if there is any easy way, is to hold your ground (position) while quickly taking your racquet back high. Just as with any other ground stroke, your goal is to get the racquet back into position before the ball crosses the net. Then, using a straight backswing, take the racquet back and high so that the racquet is above the projected height of the bounce. Step into the ball, putting some underspin on it.

In hitting this type of high ground stroke you are on the defense. Your objectives are first, to keep the ball in play, and second, to keep it as deep as possible so that your opponent won't be able to take advantage and move in.

Another way to hit a high ground stroke is to back up quickly with your racquet in position, getting back far enough so that you can take your normal swing. You should hit the ball at about waist high. This technique can only be used if you have good anticipation and quick footwork. When you get into position you can then hit your normal offensive return. If you beat the ball back you can do anything your ability will allow you to do such as lob, go for a passing shot, or hit your normal shot.

The last technique, and most offensive approach to a high ground stroke, is to move into the ball, attenpting to hit the ball on the rise before it can get too high. It will be similar to a half volley. The same basics are also applied here. As you turn your shoulder toward the net the racquet comes back immediately. Then as you move in, your racquet is prepared. Be sure to halt your momentum for just a split second before you make contact with the ball. In other words, using your split-step, you hit the ball and put a little underspin on it for control. As soon as you see the ball coming, you should decide what tactic you will employ. Actually before the match begins, you should decide what you will do if you get a high ground stroke in a particular situation.

All three techniques should be practiced, and while being practiced should be put into practice drills. You will have to really concentrate on the ball, due to the different flight pattern of the ball. If you are not used to seeing balls with high bounce, it is easy to lose your concentration.

High Forehand Ground Stroke

A. Assume ready position. B. Move to the ball as your racquet goes back. C. Get in position to hit the ball with the racquet and body prepared. D. Hit the ball. E. Follow-through.

A   B

C

D

E

The most asked questions about high ground strokes

1. Why do my high ground strokes always go into the net?
Answer: In most cases it is because you are out of position, as well as being in an awkward position. This means you are unable to prepare properly and get set for the shot. When you aren't set for a shot, you will inevitably lose power and control. To eliminate this problem, watch the flight of the ball so that you can prepare as soon as possible, and get a good step into the ball so that you meet the ball at the normal contact point.

2. Why do my high ground strokes always go long?
Answer: The answer is the same for almost any stroke that goes long. You are too slow reacting, and you hit the ball late with your racquet face open.

Approach Shots

THE APPROACH SHOT is one of the most important shots in the game. If yours is an attacking style of game, your approach shot is your third most important shot behind your serve and service return. Unfortunately, it is another one of those rarely practiced strokes.

An approach shot occurs after your opponent has hit a short ball. You move in to hit it, usually on the rise, as you come up to the net. The short ball is your invitation to come to the net. This shot is hit at or near the service line. If you attempt to come in on a shot hit from much deeper in the court, it is called suicide. You don't have enough time to make it to your homebase at the net, and your opponent will have plenty of time to get to the ball and set up. The main ingredient to an effective approach shot is to know the difference between an approach shot and a ground stroke.

Distinguishing the difference between a ground stroke and an approach shot does not come easily, but only after quite a bit of playing experience. A short ball will usually occur:

1. When your opponent has to hit a low ball.
2. When he is pulled wide off the court.

3. When he hits a ball late.
4. When he is forced to return a high top spin shot.
5. When he is more than five feet behind the baseline.

When you get your opponent in one of these awkward positions, anticipate: expect a short ball, one you can hit an approach shot off.

Once you know for sure that it is a short ball, move in quickly and attack. As you move forward, always be ready to change direction or to stop quickly. Have your side slightly toward the net so you will be in a better position when it is time to stop. Also, as you are closing in, have your racquet halfway back in position to start your swing. Then as you get to the ball, stop your momentum, with a split-step if necessary, just long enough to bend your knees. Then with your modified backswing about two-thirds of the way back, execute a smooth swing through the ball. Your type of swing will depend upon the type of spin you use. After you *hear* the ball leave your strings, look up and quickly proceed to the net.

Spin and placement are two other keys to an effective approach shot. If your ability permits, vary the spin on your approach shots for control and variety. The choice of spins are under, side, and top. Underspin will keep the ball low and force your opponent to hit the ball up, but it also permits the least amount of room for error. With sidespin your margin for error is greater. If hit effectively, it will pull your opponent off the court. Top spin, my choice for an approach shot, has the advantage of giving you more room for error, while at the same time it allows you to hit the ball with more pace.

The placement is even more important than spin in accomplishing an effective approach shot. It is important to mix them up so your opponent won't be able to anticipate them. Your choices are down-the-middle, crosscourt, or down-the-line. I prefer down-the-middle, though it depends on where your opponent is. Down-the-middle gives you the safest shot, most court to aim for, and lowest part of the net to hit over. At the same time, it doesn't give your opponent a lot of angle to work with. Crosscourt will also give you a lot of court to hit into and the net is again at its lowest point. It should be used if your opponent is out of position. However, if your opponent has time to get there, the angles are open to him. Down-the-line is the toughest one to hit accurately. The net is six inches higher here, and you are aiming for a smaller section of the court. It is a good selection if you hit it to your opponent's backhand, usually his weakest shot. If you are winning points consistently hitting to a particular spot, keep doing it until your opponent wins a few points. Then start mixing them up.

After you master spin and placement, you can work on pace. As with every other shot, too many players get hung up by being concerned with the pace on the ball. This is where errors occur.

Depth is another key ingredient. Your approach shot needs to land between the service line and the baseline. Otherwise your opponent will get to it too easily, and you will be at his mercy.

The steps to hitting an effective approach shot are:

1. Know ahead of time where you will place it and what spin you will use.
2. Since you are closer to the net use a modified backswing. Remember the closer you get to the net the shorter the backswing required. You need to hit the ball a shorter distance, you have less time to prepare. Most mistakes occur with the approach shot by trying to hit the ball too hard and using too big a swing.
3. Halt your momentum for a split second while making contact with the ball by doing your by-now-famous split-step.
4. Use a good follow-through, otherwise your approach shot will land too short.
5. Keep your head down until after you make contact. If you look up too early to see your great approach shot, you will find it where you don't want to—on your side of the net!
6. After hitting your approach shot, move quickly into position for your volley. Move in the direction of your approach shot. A common error is to admire your approach shot too long and fail to get into position for the volley. Remember, your volley is only as good as your approach shot, and, if your approach shots are good enough, you may never have to hit a volley.
7. Don't try to win the point with your approach shot.

The most asked questions about approach shots

1. Where is the best place to aim my approach shot?
Answer: It really depends on your ability as well as that of your opponent's. You would like to be able to place them anywhere, so your opponent won't know where they are going. However, if your opponent has a weak backhand, and you can *consistently* hit your approach shots to his backhand, you will either consistently win points or improve his backhand. If you are winning points consistently hitting

Approach Shot

A. Ready position is behind the baseline. B. The player sees it will be a short ball, just right for an approach shot, so she moves in quickly, with her racquet prepared. C. She halts her momentum just long enough to get her body under control, as she prepares to hit her approach shot using an abbreviated backswing. D. She leans forward making contact with the ball well out in front of her. E. Having hit the ball, she finishes with a nice follow-through. Now she is ready to proceed quickly to the net.

A

B

C

D   **E**

your approaches to a particular spot, why change? When your opponent starts to win more points than you off your approach shot,
then is the time to start mixing up your placements.

2. How big a swing should I use for my approach shots?
Answer: This answer will also depend upon your ability. In most cases
you only need half a backswing or at the most two-thirds of one for
the reasons already mentioned. Only if you play every day so that the
ability is there, can you attempt to take a larger swing.

3. Why do my approach shots usually go into the net?
Answer: This might be due to any one of the following: looking up
too early; trying to get up to the net too quickly; not getting under
the ball; or just trying to hit it too good. Concentrate only on your
approach shot and give yourself no room for error.

4. Why do my approach shots go long?
Answer: Again you have many reasons to choose from: one, you are
not putting any spin on the ball; two, you are hitting it late with your
racquet face open; three, you are taking too big a swing; or four, you
are trying to hit a shot beyond your capabilities.

99

The Volley

A VOLLEY IS A BALL HIT in the air before it bounces from anywhere on the court. A good crisp volley is a requirement for any player who wants an attacking game, or who just wants to improve his overall game. Mechanically speaking the volley is the *easiest* stroke in the game, but the execution of it is difficult for most players.

The first aspect you must conquer is your "fear" at the net. This fear is caused by being afraid of getting hit by the ball. This is natural. Unfortunately, you will get hit occasionally, that's just part of the game. With luck it won't be serious. Most serious eye injuries at the net are caused by improper stroke technique when the ball bounces off your racquet due to hitting it late. Once you overcome your fear, the volley will be much easier. To do this, start out slowly and easily. Once you gain confidence, you can increase the pace on the balls coming toward you.

Think of a volley as if you were going to catch the ball on the strings of your racquet. A good way to teach the volley is by throwing balls to a player at the net and having him catch them with one hand. This will show the player where he should make contact with the ball on his volleys. If you are at all familiar with the game of baseball, picture yourself as a first baseman stretching out for the ball. This is how you should look when executing a solid volley.

The racquet movement involved with the volley is the *easiest* of all strokes since very little racquet movement is involved. Your racquet should start in a high ready position, compared to the relatively low one for ground strokes. The racquet should be up about nose level and in the middle of your body, as opposed to favoring one side. It should be held out away from the body in a semi-comfortable position. If you get too comfortable you won't be able to react quickly enough. The racquet stays out in front of the body *throughout* the stroke. If you wanted to, you should be able to look through your strings during the entire stroke. From your ready position you simply turn your racquet face toward the on-coming ball, and while doing so, turn your shoulders slightly. Remember, the more you turn your shoulders, the farther the racquet comes back. Believe it or not that is all the racquet

100

movement you will ever need. The reason so many players have difficulty executing a solid volley is that they try to do more movement with the racquet. Depending on your ability level, if the ball is coming slowly enough, you can employ a little "push" or "punch" through the ball. When attempting a volley, keep this concept in mind; your racquet is the target for the ball, if you move the target it is harder for the ball to find its mark.

Throughout the entire stroke you should have a firm wrist and grip. The reason for the shorter and quicker stroke is that you are close to the net and the ball gets to you sooner, so your reaction time is slower. Another reason for this compact motion is that all the power you need in this stroke is already on the ball, you don't need to apply any additional force. The source of this power lies in the fact that the ball does not have to travel as far as if you were at the baseline, and the ball will not slow down any since it will not be bouncing off the court. Ask yourself this question: what happens when you hit the ball against a wall hard or easy? Which comes back harder? Answer: obviously the ball that was hit harder comes back harder. That was simple enough, but now ask yourself why? If the wall didn't move, and lets hope not, then the conclusion is that the power must have already been on the ball. Sound logical?

During a volley your feet actually do most of the work. In your ready position, you should be on the balls of your feet, and they should be as active as possible, even bouncing. If you are on the balls of your feet, you are able to move more quickly, and, in this position, you should lean forward slightly. This will make it harder to take a big backswing. Throughout the stroke your knees should be slightly bent. Every once in a while students will say they can't bend their knees. I reply, "How then do you eat your meals? Standing up?" As with any other stroke, you want your momentum to be moving forward. The volley is no exception. You should try to get in one step forward at least before making contact with the ball. You should step into the ball with the opposite foot from the side the ball is on. One way to help you move forward is to try to make contact with the ball *before* it crosses the net. Don't really do this or you will lose the point. This movement will generate more than enough power without the need to swing.

Forehand Volley

A. Player is in a good ready position. B. She has turned slightly so that her right shoulder is toward the net, while keeping the racquet out in front of her. C. She is ready to make contact with the ball when it is even with her front foot. D. After making contact she follows through in the direction she wants the ball to go. Keep in mind that the racquet must finish the follow-through on the same level or plane on which it started.

A

B

C   D

This player demonstrates how you might look when you hit a forehand volley late.

Backhand Volley

A. Ready postion at the net. B Turn slightly, keeping the racquet well out in front of you. C. Make contact with the ball when it is well out in front of you. D. Follow through with your racquet on the same level as when you hit the ball.

A

B

C

D

High Backhand Volley

The same technique applies to the backhand side. A. Player is in good ready position. B. He turns slightly, keeping his racquet out in front of him. C. Side to the net, he has just made contact with the ball with it well in front of his leading foot. D. He follows through keeping his racquet on the same level as it was when he made contact with the ball.

A

B

C

D

Your homebase for your volleys should be approximately halfway between the net and the service line. You will hit some volleys elsewhere in the court, but that usually happens when you are out of position. The reason for your homebase here is that if you are any closer, your reaction time is cut considerably, plus it is much easier for your opponent to execute a successful lob.

A low volley is a volley you are forced to hit when the ball gets below net height. Obviously when this happens you are on the defense, so play it safe. If you always move forward on your volleys, this type of shot won't occur often. To execute a low volley you first need to bend your knees so that you can get your body down to the level of the ball. If you just drop your racquet down, the face of your racquet will be open, causing the ball to be popped up. A good strategy when you see someone about ready to hit a low volley, is to move into the net so you can pick off the ball and hit the ball down to them. This will result in either winning the point or putting your opponent on the defense. A good point to remember for a low volley or any volley is to try to keep your racquet face parallel, even with your face.

Low Volley

A. Assume ready position. B. When you see the ball will be low, prepare for it with an abbreviated backswing. C. Meet the ball out front, even with your right foot. D. Finish with a follow-through.

A   B

108

C D

When hitting a low volley you have three options open to you. Your ability level will determine which one you use. You can block it back deep without any pace, the safest way to play it. Or you can try a drop volley, which is probably the hardest way. And last, you can block the ball back but with a bit of underspin to keep it low after it bounces. If you choose the latter approach, you won't be so much on the defensive.

The spin employed on most volleys should be a little underspin for control. This will help keep the ball in the court.

One reason so many players have trouble with their volleys is that they are out of position. The only key point to remember is to "follow the ball" laterally. This way you can cover the "angle of probable return." It won't always hold true, but it works 90 percent of the time. Here are a couple of staggering figures to keep in mind. 25 percent of first volleys are errors, and only 50 percent of first volleys are returned. You can see how important your first volley is.

The Angle of Probable Return

Footwork, anticipation, and knowing where to be on the tennis court are all very important elements of your tennis game. This illustration will help you visualize what it means to move toward the ball to cover the angles of probable return. Probable return refers to the area of the court to which the ball *should* be returned. *Should* is the key word. It won't always work out that way, but it will 90 percent of the time. Either at the net position or behind the baseline, position yourself between the lines of A, B, or C, depending upon which area you hit the ball to. This way you will be in perfect position to cover the return.

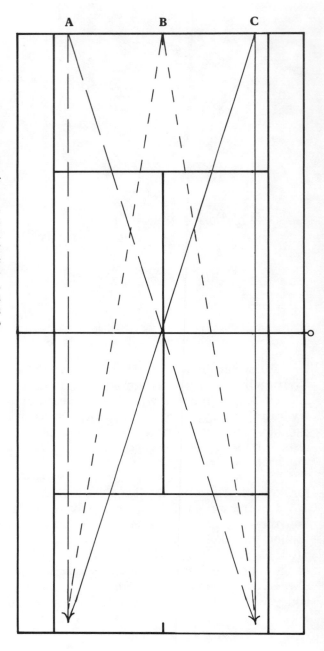

The most asked questions about volleys

1. How can I get more power into my volleys?
Answer: First of all, remember more power comes after you have good control. If you want added power on your volleys, you should make sure your wrist, grip, and arm are firm on contact. Also be sure to hit the ball on the sweet spot, meet the ball out in front of you, and get your body into the shot by getting a good step forward. If the ball is coming slowly, then, and only then, should you take a slightly longer backswing.

2. How can I avoid taking too big a backswing?
Answer: This is probably the biggest problem most players have with their volleys. They don't realize that a big backswing causes more errors than anything else. To avoid this serious problem keep your weight forward, and if that doesn't help you will have to resort to using the "fence" approach. This involves going to one of the fences surrounding the court and having a friend toss balls to you with you standing up against the fence. If you happen to take a larger than needed backswing, your racquet will pay the price. You can also do the "close order" volley drill. Here both player are at the net. When you volley from this position you don't have time for a big swing.

3. Is it legal to reach over the net to hit a volley?
Answer: It is illegal to reach over the net to hit any kind of stroke. However, it is legal to hit a volley or any other stroke and then have your follow-through pass through the plane of the net, as long as the net is not touched by your racquet or any part of your body. Believe it or not, there is an exception to this rule which I will tell you later.

4. What causes me to mis-hit my volleys?
Answer: Mis-hitting a volley, or any stroke for that matter, is usually caused by one of these four things, not having a firm grip, using too big a back swing, eyes not on the same plane as the ball, or looking up too early to admire the shot.

5. Why am I constantly hitting my volleys late?
Answer: There is no excuse for hitting a volley late, since it is mechanically the easiest stroke in the game. A lot of players have this problem. In most cases the problem is in the backswing. It is too big.

If this is not the case with you, make sure you are not positioning yourself too close to the net, that you have the correct ready position, and that you are watching the ball come off your opponent's racquet. Even if you are doing these things correctly, you might have slightly slow reflexes. If this is the problem, practice volleying with a friend at your homebases. If you do this long enough your reflex time is bound to improve.

6. Why do my volleys go into the net?
Answer: Remember if you have to make any kind of mistake, you want it to be long. I hate to report that most volley errors are into the net. To avoid being one of the statistics, make sure you aim your volleys deep into the court. You want them to land between the service line and baseline. However, if they do happen to hit the net, make sure you are not putting too much underspin on the ball, your racquet face is pointing down, and that on your follow-through your racquet comes down. Also remember where you are on the court. Too often we think we are closer to the net than we really are, and then, if we use the same stroke that we would near the net, the ball almost has to go into the net.

7. Why do my volleys go long?
Answer: We usually think we are John McEnroe or Martina Navratilova, who can aim near the lines and come out on top. However, when you and I do it the court seems to shrink and the ball goes long. In other words, don't aim so deep, your prime objective is to keep the ball in play. If this does not apply to you, then either the face of your racquet is open on contact due to hitting the ball late, or you are not putting sufficient underspin on the ball.

Half Volley

THE HALF VOLLEY IS another one of those difficult, unavoidable shots of the game. The difficulty lies in the fact you are hitting the ball on the rise, only a couple of inches above the court surface, you make contact with the ball well below the level of the net, and you are out of position while attempting to hit. You usually find yourself near the service line when attempting these. However, if you find yourself hitting too many of these near the baseline, move your homebase back a few feet.

Due to being out of position, this shot is considered a defensive one and should be dealt with as such. Your main goal with a half volley is to get it back into play any way you can, and if at all possible, as deep as you can, so your opponent can't do much with it.

The technique involved in executing a good half volley is basically simple, though we find ourselves having problems with half volleys when we try to do too much with them. So with this stroke remember to keep it as simple as possible. Since you have relatively little time to prepare for this shot, an abbreviated backswing is a must. The racquet only needs to come halfway back to give you sufficient power, because you are closer to the net and have less time to prepare. You will see that the mechanics of the stroke are very similar to those of a regular volley. As soon as you see the ball on top of you, quickly rotate your shoulders slightly, taking your racquet back just halfway. Bend your knees so you can get down to the level of the ball. Then as you step forward and meet the ball, straighten up and lift the ball over the net. Finish with a normal follow-through. A split-step will help eliminate some of the problems with your half volley, since it helps you to get your body under control.

The most asked questions about the half volley

1. How can I get more depth on my half volley?
Answer: In order to get more depth you will need to open the face of your racquet very slightly. Also, be sure to have your normal follow-through, without which you will lose considerable depth.

2. Why do most of my half volleys go into the net?
Answer: In most cases when this happens, you are trying to rush the stroke too much. If you hurry it too much, there won't be another one to get ready for because you will find the ball in the net. Whenever you rush a stroke you are taking your eyes off the ball too early, while at the same time pulling your racquet out of position. The ball also finds its way into the net quite often when you try to hit too good a half volley. Remember this stroke is defensive in nature, so play it safe and win more points.

113

Half Volley

A. The player moves up to the net, racquet up and out in front, ready for anything. B. He sees that he will have to hit a half volley and starts the backswing, as he begins to get down on the ball. C. He has completed his abbreviated backswing and is ready to make contact with the ball. D. The player makes contact with the ball, hitting it when it is even with his front foot while carefully watching the ball. E. He hits through the ball, keeping the racquet in the hitting zone, with his eyes still fixed on the contact point. F. He follows through the ball and rises slightly to lift the ball over the net. Now he is ready to move up to the net.

A

B

C

D

E

F

Drop Volley

THE DROP VOLLEY or stop volley, as it is sometimes called, is a very delicate volleying stroke. The object is to take the speed off your opponent's ball by gently caressing it so that it barely drops over the net. This difficult shot can be hit on either the forehand or backhand side.

Before you try to execute a drop volley, you need to know which balls are candidates for a drop volley. You are looking for a ball hit at medium pace, not too far away from you. In other words, you want one that is set up and asking to be dropped over.

Your ready position should look like any other volley. Remember, disguise is the key with this shot. If you smile too much, your opponent will be able to read the shot and will be able to get to it in plenty of time. Then watch out!

As soon as you see the ball approaching, immediately turn your shoulders and racquet face to the net. Then, with your very abbreviated backswing, take a good step forward. With this stroke you want to relax your usual firm grip on the racquet, and with an easy downward cupping action, take the speed off the ball.

As with a drop shot, your goal is to have your drop volley bounce at least three times before it gets to your opponent's service line.

The drop volley can be a very effective offensive weapon, but if not hit accurately it can spell disaster. In my opinion drop volleys are not hit enough. I feel they should be nearly one-third of your volleys. This will enable you to keep your opponent off guard so he can't camp out at the baseline. It will also wear him out trying to get to them.

The two main mistakes in executing an effective drop volley are:

1. Trying to make the shot too good.
2. Choosing the wrong balls to hit.

If possible when hitting a drop volley, angle it away from your opponent. That way he will have to run much farther for the ball.

A drop volley is usually recommended for advanced players, but

116

beginners can have fun with them, too. If you are just starting out, don't expect too much from them because they can be very frustrating. Both beginners and advanced players need to spend considerably more time practicing this unique stroke.

Drop Volley

A. Assume a good ready position. B. Turn slightly, keeping your racquet in front of you. C. Make contact with the ball when it is even with your right foot. Note that the grip for a drop volley is slightly relaxed. D. When following through on a drop volley, "cup" under the ball in order to take speed off of it.

A

B

117

C

D

The most asked questions about the drop volley

1. What causes my drop volley to go into the net?
Answer: Usually it is because you are trying to execute the "perfect" drop volley either by taking too much speed off the ball, or by aiming too close to the net. Only by practicing will you find the right combination.

2. How can I stop being attacked every time I hit a drop volley too deep?
Answer: That is simple—don't hit any more drop volleys! Now for the right answer. If you want to stop becoming a human target, avoid having the racquet face open on contact, and don't choose the wrong balls off which to hit a drop volley.

Lob Volley

THE LOB VOLLEY is another one in the category of touch shots. This means you need to be able to feel the ball on your strings throughout the stroke. For this reason this shot is recommended for only advanced players. The not-so-advanced players can attempt it but should be careful. This offensive maneuver will either be a spectacular outright winner, or you will be running for cover.

This shot is only attempted when everyone is at the net. It is another good way to mix up your game and keep your opponent off guard.

Disguise is also the key ingredient for this shot, for if your opponent sees it coming you will be in trouble. Your ready position should resemble that of your regular volley, then when you are in the middle of a quick volley exchange just slightly open the face of your racquet, and with your usual firm wrist and grip, lift the ball deep behind your opponent. Your follow-through should be in an upward motion finishing above your head.

This difficult shot can be attempted in either doubles or singles. Hit this unique shot off your best volleying side. Also if possible, hit it over your opponent's backhand side. That way if he does get it, he can't do as much with it. Before attempting this, the most dangerous shot in the game, spend some time practicing it.

Lob Volley

A. Player stands in good ready position. B. He turns slightly and opens up the face of the racquet. C. This is right after contact with the ball—notice the open angle of the racquet face. D. He completes the shot with a high follow-through for added depth.

A

B

C

D

The most asked question about the lob volley

1. The only question I have been asked concerning this stroke has been: In which direction do I run for cover after I attempt a volley lob?

Answer: If that is your question, too, then you are hitting your lob volleys too short. To prevent this from occurring, open the face of your racquet a little more than normal and make sure you follow through. If at all possible, aim your lob volley over the backhand side of your opponent. At least then, if your lob volley is short, he won't be able to hurt you as much.

Body Volley

ANOTHER TYPE OF VOLLEY, commonly used as a last resort, is the body volley. This occurs when your opponent has misdirected a ball toward your navel. In most cases it isn't intentional, at least let's hope so.

When most players see this ball coming, their first reaction is panic either from not knowing what to do or just plain fright! Being frightened is common and may be with you forever, but from now on there should be no excuses for not knowing what to do. Some of these volleys can be prevented by having a good moving ready position near the net and following the ball closely with your eyes and feet.

You actually don't have much choice in how you return one ball. A forehand volley is almost impossible in this situation. Your only alternative is a backhand volley because you don't usually have time to get out of the way.

If you attempt a forehand volley you should take at least two steps before executing a crisp volley. If you use a backhand volley, you are already in position.

Once you detect that the ball is on a collision course with your body, immediately take one step to the side and forward to get out of the way. In most cases you won't have time for your abbreviated backswing because you will be caught off guard. Make sure your racquet is out in front of your body, not just for protection, but it also will allow you to hit a crisp volley. Try to meet the ball as far out in front of you as possible, and of course, have a good follow-through.

As with any stroke, this one should be practiced. Have a friend start out by just throwing balls easily at you so you can work on your technique. This way the fear shouldn't be as great in a game situation.

Body Volley

A. This is a good ready position. B. The best method of hitting a body volley is a backhand volley. The ball is hit in front of the body. C. If you try to hit a body volley with a forehand, it is almost impossible to move out of the way of the ball and still have time to hit it in front of you.

A

B

C

The Overhead Smash

THE OVERHEAD SMASH IS one of the most spectacular shots in the game, even if it is missed. It is an important stroke to have in your arsenal, if you are going to improve your level of play. An overhead smash is a confidence shot. As a lob goes up you should be ready to put it away. At the net, you should be hoping for a lob, not dreading one. It is a shot seldom practiced, though it should be practiced often.

From a technical standpoint the overhead smash is similar to the serve, though abbreviated and demanding more intricate timing. When you are at the net and see a lob go up, immediately turn your side to the net and drop the racquet behind your back. To turn sideways all you need to do is step back with your right foot, if you're right-handed and vice versa if left-handed. To bring the racquet back, just drop it over your shoulder and relax your grip. There will not be enough time to take your full backswing. That's the easy part—now comes the hard part.

Next you move your feet to get into position. Unlike the serve, where you are always in position, with the overhead you need to constantly adjust your feet so that you can make contact with the ball when it is in front of you.

Except for watching the ball, the rest is just a matter of timing. If a player has a weak overhead it is usually a case of misjudging the ball. As the ball gets closer to you it picks up speed. This makes it harder to time. So remember to swing *earlier* than you think you have to, to make up for the increase in speed of the ball. Make sure you reach up for the ball and snap your wrist just as you do in the serve.

The grip you use should be the same you use in the serve, either an eastern forehand or preferably, a continental. For more control you might try putting some spin on your overhead smash. If you are reaching up for the ball, you will naturally put a little top spin on the ball. Experiment and try to put on some sidespin or slice on the ball. Utilizing slice will pull your opponent off the court, and you won't have to hit the ball quite so hard. When your ability permits, mix up the placements of your overheads. An opponent can quickly realize if all your smashes go to the same place on the court. To play it safe aim either down the middle or crosscourt allowing yourself the greatest

125

room for error. Accurate placement is always more important than power.

If the lob has a low trajectory, it is advisable to hit the overhead before it bounces. If the lob is either very high or deep in the court, it is wiser to let the ball bounce first. The timing will be easier, even though it will give your opponent more time to get prepared.

When you practice your overhead smashes, practice them from all parts of the court and with various degrees of difficulty. It is also a good idea to practice hitting top spin lobs. Jump up for these and try to snap your wrist. In most cases all you can do is just block the ball back into the court. On all overheads try not to leave the court or jump at the ball. If you do you lose your balance and control.

The Overhead

A. This player is in the classic ready position, ready for either an overhead or volley. B. Immediately after detecting that it is an overhead, she turns her side to the net and begins to drop the racquet into position. C. Now she is in the "power position"—ready to make any final adjustments to the ball. D. She reaches up for the ball, hitting it with her arm extended out in front of her. E. This is the follow-through.

A

126

B

C

D

E

The key elements to an effective overhead smash are:

1. Prepare early.
2. Keep your head up.
3. Reach up before you think you have to.
4. Control first, then power.
5. Keep the ball in front of you.

If by some chance you whiff the overhead, don't give up. You still have time to recover and make a shot. In this situation your only hope is one of your closet shots. Pull one out of storage and give it a try. You have nothing to lose, and it could just be the shot to sway the momentum your way.

Whether it is hit for a winner or "whiffed," the overhead is one of the most spectacular shots of the game. In this case it was whiffed for the most common reason—the player looked down to admire his shot too early.

While playing and especially while hitting overheads, you have to be aware of the position of the sun. If the sun is in your eyes while you attempt an overhead, you can either put your other hand up to shade your eyes or let the ball bounce before you hit it.

Along with the overhead smash, mention must be given to the backhand overhead. If your opponents are good players this is where some of their lobs should be aimed. For this reason this stroke should be worked on. For this stroke use the same grip you use with your backhand volley, turn your side to the net, take your racquet back high, and while watching the ball carefully, reach up and snap your wrist. Most errors with this stroke occur when balls go into the net. The reasons for the net balls are: you try to hit them too hard, aim too short, look away too early to get ready for the next shot, or you forget where you are on the court.

The most asked questions about overheads

1. Why do I mis-hit so many overheads?
Answer: The overhead is the easiest stroke in the game to mis-hit because of timing. To avoid too many mistakes you need to practice the stroke. When you're practicing keep these points in mind: shorten your backswing, keep your head up, reach up earlier than you think you have to, and move your feet quickly so you can be in position to hit the ball out in front of you. If you look down too early to see your winner, you won't have to look far—it will be in the net.

2. How can I get more power on my overhead?
Answer: After you have mastered the control element, and you want some added power, this is what you want to make sure you are doing right: meet the ball out in front of your body, reach up for the ball, keep your head up so you can hit the ball on the sweet spot, snap your wrist through the ball, and have a good follow-through.

3. Should I use spin on my overheads?
Answer: Spin will give you more control and deception on any stroke and the overhead is no exception. If you are reaching up more for the ball you are automatically putting top spin on on the ball. Also experiment by hitting your overhead with a little slice spin. This will pull your opponent out of position, and set you up if another shot is needed to finish the point.

4. What should I do if my opponent is about ready to hit an overhead?
Answer: When you see your opponent smiling as he gets ready to hit his overhead, it is your clue to back up immediately so that you are at least three to four feet behind the baseline. That way you should have sufficient time to prepare for the return. If your opponent always hits his overheads to one spot on the court, or if you think you know where the ball will go, you can anticipate and move a couple of steps in that direction. Otherwise, your only hope is that he will miss the overhead. Be sure to be on the balls of your feet so you can react quickly.

Lobs

THE LOB IS PROBABLY the most underrated and least used shot in the game. A fair analogy of a lob can be summed up by this question that I heard a pro ask his class, "How is a lob like religion?" Answer: "It is seldom practiced, but you turn to it in time of need." I don't feel this is true with religion, though it describes a lob perfectly.

The reason it is seldom used is that the stroke is rarely practiced. If that is the case how can you expect to use it in a game situation? Most players aren't aware of its advantages. The advantages of a lob are:

1. It is a good change of pace shot.
2. When you are out of position, it can buy you time to get back to your homebase.
3. It can force the net rusher to hit an overhead, one of the hardest shots in the game, or make him retreat to the baseline.
4. It can be used to hit an out-right winner.
5. It is easier to execute than passing shots.
6. It's a good percentage shot.
7. If your opponent is facing the sun, a lob forces him to look into the sun.

Heights for Offensive and Defensive Lobs

When executing an offensive lob, your aim is to win the point outright (immediately). For this reason the trajectory (height) isn't great—usually about thirteen feet. You hit a defensive lob when you are out of position to give you time to recover and get back into position. The height of defensive lobs range from twenty feet on up.

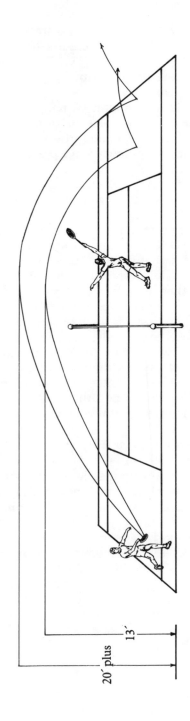

20' plus

13'

A lob can be described as a stroke in which the ball is lifted high into the air. In order to accomplish this you need to:

1. Use the proper grip.
2. Prepare early.
3. Use a low to high swing.
4. Open the face of your racquet.
5. Use an exaggerated upward follow-through.
6. Practice, practice, and practice.

To make your lobs effective you must disguise them. You want your opponent to think you are going for a passing shot until the last moment.

In order to execute an effective lob, it is necessary to decide as soon as possible that this is the shot you want to attempt. Once you decide, don't change your mind. If you do change your mind, it is usually too late. Then you end up hitting an "in-between" shot, something that resembles both a lob and a ground stroke. And you're right, it usually ends up on your side of the net.

When you decide to lob, get your racquet back into position early. Since disguise is the key and you want your opponent to expect a ground stroke, try not to do anything out of the ordinary. A smile is a sure giveaway. At the appropriate time start your forward swing from low to high. When you meet the ball your racquet face should be open. The more open the more defensive the lob and the higher it will go. Be sure to hit through the ball and finish with a high follow-through.

If you are a so-called beginner, aim your lobs down the middle of the court. This will give you more room for error. More advanced players should mix up the placements of their lobs, hit some crosscourt and others over the opponent's backhand side. That way even if he does reach it he won't be able to do much with it.

There are two types of lobs, the typical defensive lob and the lesser, and more dangerous, offensive lob. The defensive lob is hit fairly high for the previously mentioned reasons. A good lob will land between the service line and the baseline.

Your objective in hitting an offensive lob is to win the point outright. The only difference between these two lobs is the trajectory. The offensive lob is hit harder with a lower arch, preferably over your opponent's backhand side. That way if he does reach it he won't be able to make a good return.

132

The Lob

A. This player is in good ready position. B. He has pivoted and turned his side to the net and is beginning to move toward the ball. The racquet has already begun to move into position. C. He has reached the ball, the racquet is prepared, and he is about to step into the ball. D. He has stepped into the ball, meeting it when it is even with his lead foot. Notice the open face of the racquet. E. He has just finished his follow-through. His eyes are still focused on the contact point. He is not looking up to admire his stroke.

A

B

C

D

E

Returning a Lob

Believe it or not there is a specific technique to returning a lob. This is another one of those shots that is not used until it is needed in a game, and then it's too late unless you have practiced. Simply put, this is the shot you have to hit when the ball gets behind you. To avoid this shot never let the ball get behind you. That is impossible if you play any kind of an attacking game.

The same basic technique is used on both sides. As soon as you see that the ball is going to go over your head, turn quickly and run in a semi-circular pattern, keeping your eyes on the ball, with your racquet already prepared so when you get to the ball, you are ready to hit it. Your goal is to beat the ball back, then stop and be able to step into the ball. If you can do this you can hit an offensive shot. Otherwise, you will have to improvise by pulling out one of your closet shots again. Your best percentage shot in this situation is to hit a defensive lob. The reason for not running a straight pattern back to the ball is that you would end up too close to the ball, be unable to hit a good shot, and possibly get hit by the lob.

If you are caught with an offensive lob going over your head, pray a lot. It is almost impossible to run one down. Don't give up without trying. You have to make some attempt to get the ball. Who knows, you may just win the point!

Top Spin Lob

The top spin lob is the most popular lob today, even though it is the hardest type to execute. It became popular at the same time the top spin ground stroke did.

Technically it is basically the same as a regular offensive lob. Prepare early by getting your racquet back before the ball crosses the net. As you bring your racquet through the hitting zone, be sure to keep your racquet face parallel to the net. As you hit through the ball, concentrate on brushing up the back side from low to high and finish with a nice high follow-through. Think of it as hitting a high top spin ground stroke. You will need to hit a top spin lob harder than a regular lob due to all the spin on the ball. Otherwise the lob will land too short, if it makes it over the net at all.

The stroke will take a lot of practice to master due to the added top spin on the ball, but it will be well worth the effort. If hit effec-

Returning a Lob

A. Player is in a ready position at the net. B. She realizes she will not be able to hit a volley or an overhead and will be forced to run down the lob. C. She runs back with her racquet prepared. D. She has won her race against the ball and beaten it back. Notice she is in the correct relationship to the ball—not too close to it. E. Since she got back before the ball, she was able to step into the ball and meet it when it was even with her front foot. F. She finishes her follow-through.

A

B

C

D

E

F

tively, it will be an outright winner. The top spin on the ball will make it literally impossible to run down, once it hits the court.

So try it and have some fun with it, I think you'll enjoy it. I would recommend that you be able to execute the two other types of lobs first before attempting this more advanced type.

The most asked questions about lobs

1. Why do my lobs usually land short?
Answer: When your lobs land short it is because of a lack of a long, high follow-through. Other reasons could be: not allowing for the wind; aiming too short and, if you are deep behind the baseline and attempt to hit a top spin lob, failing to hit it hard enough. Top spin lobs must be hit harder to compensate for the added spin on the ball.

2. Why do my lobs land long?
Answer: Are you aiming for the lines again? If that is not the case, did you consider the wind? In most cases, if a lob goes long you are just aiming too deep. For this reason, aim your lobs over the net and not over the player at the net, as most players do. By this I mean the apex or the highest part of the lob's arc is above the net. Remember the main objective is to get the ball back into play, and make your opponenet hit the ball to win the point.

Dropshots

THE DROPSHOT IS JUST ONE in the catagory of "touch" shots. The dropshot is defined as "a stroke made with a sharp lift of the racquet as it meets the ball, which makes the ball twist forward rapidly and drop unnaturally after it crosses the net."* To be able to hit a good dropshot you must have a good feel for the ball.

It is not wise to hit dropshots off all balls. The ball should come at a slow or medium pace, otherwise, the shot is too hard to execute. You should know when to hit a dropshot. Some authors say to use them only when you have a big lead or are far behind. I agree with

* *Official Encyclopedia of Tennis*, Harper & Row, P. 461.

Dropshot

A. Assume ready position by doing a split-step. B. Move to the ball using a short backswing. C. Make contact with the ball with the racquet face slightly open. D. Follow through with your eyes still focusing on the point of contact.

A

B

C

D

this if you never practice the shot. Otherwise, a dropshot can be good weapon to use and should be used often.

You will find that disguise is one of the keys to hitting a good dropshot. You want your opponent to believe you are going to hit your normal ground stroke, then at the last moment, you hit the dropshot and catch him off guard.

The dropshot is generally considered a low percentage shot. If you hit it too deep, your opponent will be set up for any easy winner. If you are in the wrong position to hit a good one, it will be ineffective. You must practice this shot. The reasons for attempting a dropshot are:

1. If you're playing against a poor volleyer, this will make him come to the net.
2. If your opponent is playing too far behind the baseline, he will have a long way to run for the ball.
3. If your opponent has poor footwork.
4. For a change of pace.
5. To let your opponent know you have a dropshot, so he won't be able to camp at the baseline.
6. To tire out your opponent.
7. They're fun!

There are two types of dropshots which you should have in your arsenal. The first is one you hit from just inside the baseline. If you attempt one from any farther back the odds for making a good one are against you, and your opponent will have plenty of time to react to it. This shot is employed only to draw your opponent to the net and not to hit an outright winner. Then your opponent will have to test his or her volleying skills. You can move your opponent around even more then by hitting a lob.

The second type of dropshot is the one when we go for an outright winner. This shot should only be attempted when you are near the service line. It should usually be directed toward the opposite side from where your opponent is. A good drop shot should bounce at least *three* times before it gets to the service line. If it bounces less, it will be too deep and too easy to get to. Most dropshots are hit crosscourt because the net is lower in the middle, you have more court available for a good shot, and you have the angles working for you.

If your opponent has a dropshot be ready to anticipate it. If you expect one, move a couple of steps inside your baseline so you will be in position to run it down. A good strategy is to return a dropshot with one of your own, unless the dropshot is too deep. The answer to any problems you might have with your dropshots will be the same as for the drop volleys.*

Passing Shots

A PASSING SHOT IS a stroke hit past you or your opponent. The player is unable to return the ball as it lands inside the court. A passing shot is used when a player or players are at the net. Be sure to mix up your shots. If you hit them all to the same place, your opponent will be able to anticipate and get there in time. There are three places open to you to aim your passing shots: crosscourt, down-the-line, or right at the net person's navel. When you hit your shot be sure to keep it low over the net and put enough spin on the ball to keep it in the court. Aim for the service lines, otherwise the ball has a tendency to float too much and can easily be picked off.

    Decide early where you want to hit your shot and don't change your mind. Have enough confidence in your shots to keep your head down throughout the stroke.

Closet Shots

THIS PHRASE WAS COINED by the infamous Vic Braden, author, humorist and well-known tennis instructor. Closet shots are shots attempted when there is no way possible for your ability to allow you to make a good shot. These are shots you should keep in your closet and not use them on the court.

    Closet shots will vary with each player, depending on their ability level. This is where it is important to know your ability, especially under pressure. Closet shots either occur when you are out of position and are desperate, or when you just get tired and go for an outright winner. Since the name of the game is percentages, these are the shots you should not use when you are in trouble or tired.

---

* *Official Encyclopedia of Tennis,* Harper & Row, p. 461.

Heights of Ground Strokes and Passing Shots

On your ground strokes give yourself plenty of margin for error. Three feet to five feet is the recommended height. You have to play fairly close to the net for your passing shots, but not as close as some players do. Two feet behind the net is what is advised.

Examples of closet shots are:

1. A topspin lob.
2. A return of serve down the line.
3. Going for an outright winner off a return of lob.
4. Hitting an overhead smash from near the baseline before the ball bounces off a high lob.
5. Attempting a dropshot from behind the baseline.
6. Attempting a drop volley off a hard passing shot.
7. An American twist serve.
8. Going for an outright winner off a return of serve.

Remember all shots, including these, are not closet shots if you practice them.

Practicing

PRACTICE IS VERY IMPORTANT, especially if you are going to improve the level of your game. There are many techniques you can use to improve your game either by yourself or with others. The two main concerns in dealing with your practice are that you have fun and give it your total concentration. The time you spend practicing isn't as important as the effort you put into it. Or, as the old saying goes, it's not quantity but quality. As you will find, or as you have already found out, even with practice your ability level does not continue to rise like an elevator. It can be pictured better by a stair-step progression. In other words, your level of play will improve and will stay at that level for a while before it improves more. However, some players' progression charts look more like a plateau. These long plateaus usually occur when players play only once a week and don't practice in between. So practice and avoid these long plateaus.

You can't realistically expect to improve your game by only playing once a week. Besides that, it is physically unwise to engage in strenuous activity just once a week. It is much better for your heart and all your other organs to get a minimum amount of stress three times a week than overdoing it once a week.

Some methods to improve your game by yourself are:

1. Hitting against a backboard, rebound net, or garage door.
2. Using a ball machine.
3. Doing some bounce-hits.
4. Practicing your serve.
5. Doing some eye–hand coordination games.
6. Playing mirror tennis.

You need to be aware of these methods of practice, because as you know, sometimes it is hard to find someone to play or practice with.

When practicing with a backboard or ball machine, your aim is to work on consistency and grooving your strokes. With either method you are able to hit a lot of balls within a very short time. This in turn will develop what is known as "muscle memory" and "mind memory." Muscle memory refers to the specific muscle groups remembering what they need to do in order to perform a particular stroke. While mind memory relates to your mind remembering automatically what to do before you have to remind it. A good example of this is when we say to ourselves, "Get your racquet back!."

When practicing your serve, work on all the types of serves you would use in a match, including your second serve. If you don't feel you have enough balls to practice your serve, your local club may be willing to get rid of some of their older balls for a reduced rate. If a rebound net is handy, practice serving over it. You will be amazed at how well it will improve your serve.

Bounce-hits are a good way to improve your ground strokes, overheads, lobs, and even return of lobs. Using your imagination you can put yourself through some rigorous movement drills. The technique of bounce-hits is to throw or place the ball out in front of you so you can hit a good stroke. It may take a little practice to place the ball where you want it so your point of contact will be in the proper spot.

Eye–hand coordination drills involve any technique of using your racquet and eyes together to get a better feeling for the ball.

A few basic techniques are:

1. Bouncing the ball on the court using the racquet. Test your control by trying to bounce the ball on the same spot of the court.
2. Bounce the ball in the air. If you are not running all over the court with this drill then you have good control.
3. One step further is doing flip-flops. Hitting the ball in the air alternating your forehand and backhand grips.

146

4. Finally, for you hotdogs, try bouncing the ball either on the ground or in the air using the frame or butt of your racquet. This will show you what kind of control you have with your racquet and eyes.

Even though practicing by yourself is important, working out with one or more other players is of greater value. The reason is that you are in playing situations. When playing with others you inadvertently put undue pressure on yourself, pressure such as you might experience in a match. Sometimes you just like to hit, but for the most part, you need to have specific goals in mind for your practice. After warming up all your strokes, start working on the areas of your game that really need it such as backhands down the line, overheads, and returns of serve. Keep in mind that it may be more fun to practice your best strokes, but it's more important to practice your weaker strokes. The chapter on drills will cover in detail the specific drills you should use in your practice.

Just as important as practicing is to try to play as many matches as you can. No practice can really simulate what you go through under match conditions. A general rule of thumb is to play one-third of your matches against players a little weaker then yourself, another third against players of the same ability level, and the final third against players better than your ability level. While playing matches against players weaker than yourself, you can work on strokes you normally wouldn't attempt and at the same time build up your confidence. When you play against players better than yourself, you have to work harder which in itself will improve your own game. At the same time you should be loose with no fear of losing.

Practicing has to be fun. Make it fun and improve your game at the same time.

Strategy

YOUR STRATEGY IS ONLY AS GOOD as your ability to execute *one* stroke at a time. Your total attention should be directed toward that one stroke, otherwise you may not get another one. Basic strategy is simple, just get the ball back one more time than your opponent and you will win every match. I think Vic Braden, noted author and tennis

The 80 Percent Theory

Since roughly 80 percent of all balls land in the marked area, this is the area you need to cover. You should be able to cover it easily from your position behind the baseline. You should also aim your shots into this area. Aiming for the corners or lines usually spells disaster.

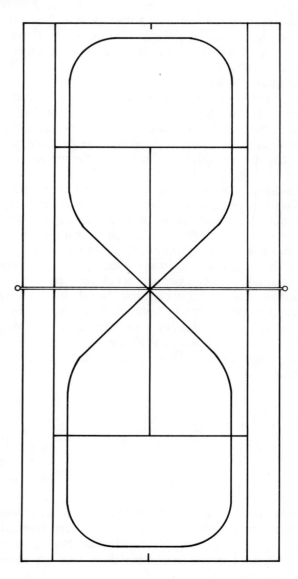

professional stated it best in his book, *Tennis for the Future,* when he said, "Learn to hit the ball down the middle and deep—that's all the strategy you'll need to beat 99 percent of the players in the world." When two players of the same ability compete then strategy can mean the difference.

The key to any type of strategy is consistency. To be consistent you must practice and be patient. Some people say, "Patience is a virtue." I feel that is especially true in tennis.

Statisticians claim that in professional matches unforced errors outnumber winners ten to one. For average players unforced errors outnumber winners by the staggering figure of thirty to one. You can see how important it is to keep the ball in play.

More often than not we get too hung up planning our complicated strategic maneuvers, when we would have been better off practicing our strokes. The more complicated the strategy the harder it is to execute, so keep your strategy simple and you will win more matches.

Your strategy should consist of playing "percentage" tennis. Percentage tennis means playing the proper shot at the right time, while staying within your capabilities. Percentage tennis will vary according to the player's style. If a player is at home behind the baseline, then hitting ground strokes is percentage tennis for him, as in the case with Bjorn Borg and Chris Evert Lloyd. If a player's best tactic is to serve and volley, then this is his style of percentage tennis. John McEnroe is a good example of this type of player. A third style is an all-around player who is at home anywhere on the court. Jimmy Connors is this type of player, and this is what I consider the best style. No matter whether you are just learning the game or an advanced player, it is important that you develop a style best suited to yourself. This style may change the more you play, or you may decide to keep your original style if it works for you. As long as you are winning with your style why change it? You don't see Chris Evert Lloyd or John McEnroe very often change their styles of attack. Why should they? They are the best in the world at what they do. However, throughout the course of a match, if you find your strategy is not working, you should be flexible enough to change your strategy. It could make a difference.

During a match we lose more points from unforced errors than we win from hitting winners. So it is our goal to cut down on the number of unforced errors by keeping the ball in play and having our opponent make the errors. Speaking of errors, most errors or points lost occur from hitting the ball into the net. For this reason we need to concentrate more on lifting the ball higher over the net. This will keep the ball nice and deep in the court.

Traffic Light or Zone Theory

The idea behind this theory is for you to know where you are on the court at all times. Too often points and matches are lost because players do not know where they are on the court. Knowing where you are is a *must* if you are going to play percentage tennis. From the backcourt or red zone, your goals are to move your opponent around while making very few errors. From this position you should *not* go for winners—the odds are just too great. In no-person's-land (formerly no-man's-land), you should be very cautious when hitting the ball. Once you hit it, try to move up to attack zone. When you get to the attack zone, "Go for it!" This is the best place from which to hit a winner.

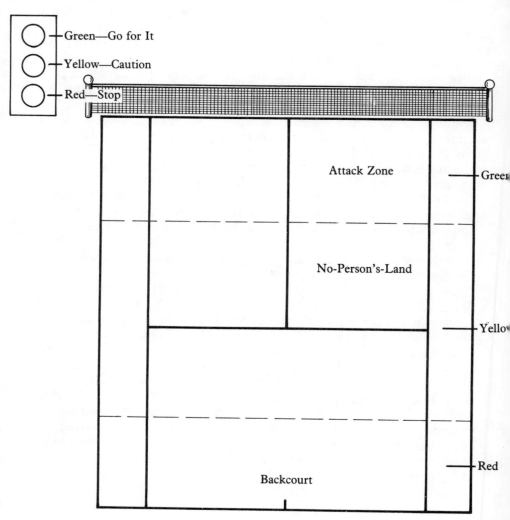

The Blanket Theory

Visualize for a minute that you are at your baseline and this is your opponent on the other side of the net. If you were to put a blanket over the net, this is what you would see—none of the court and only part of your opponent. This should reinforce the realization that the net is a fixed barrier, higher than we imagine. We should overcome this situation by "lifting" the ball over the net, because most of our errors are due to balls going into the net.

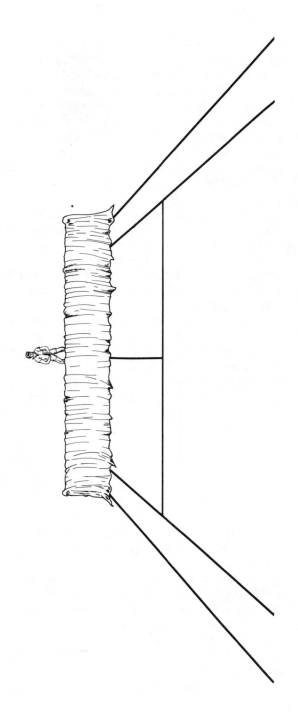

It is important that you take advantage of your strengths by hitting your best strokes, while at the same time exploiting your opponent's weaknesses. This can be done by bringing a baseline player to the net or by keeping a volleyer away. By the same token, if you have a weakness in one of your ground strokes, slightly adjust your position to compensate for it. However, don't compensate too much or your opponent will know exactly how to attack you.

Be sure to cover the crosscourt shots since they are the most commonly hit. If you find yourself in a crosscourt rally, remember that the player who changes the pattern of the ball usually loses the point.

While observing matches I have seen countless numbers of points lost, not because of stroke production, but because the player or players were out of position. What good does it do if you have a great forehand, if you find yourself out of position and unable to hit it effectively? At all times know where you are on the court, and where you should be. This sounds easier than it really is, but it is vital to a sound tennis game.

Being able to anticipate where your opponent will hit the ball, will give you a big advantage in getting into position. After playing with your opponent for a while, you should be able to have a good idea where he will hit the ball in a particular situation. Also if you know the angles of probable return and play the percentages, you will usually be in the right place at the right time.

Singles Strategy

YOUR STRATEGY IN SINGLES, as well as doubles, will be dictated by your ability. You can only do as much as your body will allow. If you are presently at the beginner level your strategy is the least complicated. When you are just starting out all you are trying to do is get the ball back anywhere in the court. Aim all strokes down the middle of the court, allowing the greatest margin for error. It would be wise for us so-called advanced players to use this strategy more often. As a beginner you are just becoming aware of what strokes you can make, so at this point in your playing career experiment with your strokes and learn just what you can do.

As you progress to the intermediate level you add more shots to

152

your arsenal. You learn the concepts of spin serves, and how they will help your game. You occasionally use the serve and volley tactic, coming in behind a good serve. Besides adding the spin serve you also add the lob to your bag of shots. At this stage of your game you begin to move your opponent around some, either laterally or up and back. While doing the above, you also improve the control and power of your regular strokes.

By the time you have reached the advanced player level you should be able to use all the strokes in the book, such as dropshot, drop volley, and top spin lob. You should be serving and returning serve and rushing as often as your playing style dictates. You have added additional spin to your strokes, while at the same time you are able to move your opponent around even more. By the end of the third game, you should have tried to employ all your strokes within your arsenal.

How many of you have lost to the "dinker" on your block? I hate to admit it, but I have. There is nothing worse than losing to a dinker, except being a dinker and losing. Dinkers are players who just "pat" the ball back, and they are good at it. With their unorthodox strokes they cause you to get frustrated and lose, because you are playing *their* game. In order to beat a dinker, you must play your own game, keep cool, and don't worry about them. Don't get me wrong, if you're a dinker you're still okay in my book, it's just your style of play I don't like.

There are two good strategies I have found beneficial in singles. One is to hit a high ground stroke to a player's weak side. While he is watching the ball, sneak into the net. The other one is when you find yourself in a baseline rally, pretend you are doing the rally quota drill. The first tactic I borrowed from Guillermo Vilas, and the latter one I learned the hard way through experience. Vilas uses this tactic to perfection and so can you. When your opponent turns his head down, this is your time to close in on the net. In most cases you will find yourself in a good position to hit a volley, if not a winning volley. Be sure not to come up too early or your opponent will know what you're up to. It is also a good idea to come up on your opponent's weakest shot, usually his backhand. All too often we get impatient during a long baseline rally. Concentrate on the ball and see how long you can keep the ball in play. To enhance your concentration, count the number of times you hit the ball, just the way you do in the rally quota drill. You will be amazed at how well this works.

Doubles Strategy

THE TWO KEYS TO SUCCESS in doubles are communication and moving together. Communication refers to letting your partner know what you are going to do and what your opponents are doing. To work together effectively it is important that your partner knows if you are going to move up to the net or stay back. In doing so it is not necessary to use complete sentences, good grammar is not one of the requirements for good, sound tennis. All you really need to say is "Up" or "Back" or "Stay" to get your message across. Before the match begins it should be decided who will cover the ground strokes up the middle from the baseline. Then there will be no need to communicate and no confusion. Usually it will be the player who will hit his forehand, since in most cases it is the stronger stroke. However, if that player has a weak forehand, forget what I just said and let the player with the backhand take it.

Since most doubles teams don't play together for a long time it is important each one know what the other one is doing. It is a good idea when you're playing doubles and one of you is left-handed to play so that both your forehands are down the middle. That is where most of the balls go.

Some tennis experts tell you that the word "yours" is not part of the tennis vocabulary. This word is usually heard when a lob goes over someone's head, usually yours. I feel that the player with the best angle should retrieve the lob, so in some cases it is perfectly all right to say it. Just don't get in the habit of saying it or using it for an excuse. If you move correctly as a doubles team, you will always know whose ball it is.

It is a good idea to let your partner know what your opponents are up to. That way he will have time to alter his shot if necessary. Such a case would be if both your opponents are rushing the net. Your partner should know his options. In this case he had better lob.

The player hitting the ball is the captain of the team for that shot. If you are lucky he knows what he is going to do, so he should be the one giving the command.

The players who make up a doubles team should move together as if a rope were tied between them. Where one goes, so should his partner. This applies to moving laterally, as well as up and back. The reasons for moving laterally together, either at the net or behind the baseline, is to protect the middle—also referred to as the California Freeway—and to cover the angle of probable return. You've probably heard the saying "there is strength in numbers." Well, this also applies to doubles and is another reason for moving to the net together. In addition, when you move to the net together you put more pressure on your opponents, and they have less court to hit into. They also have fewer options open to them, and it is harder to hit to the weaker player. With both players at the net their opponents have just two options, passing shots or lobs.

The best reason for getting to the net is that statisticians have proven that most points are won at the net. To play effective doubles you need to have a good volley and return of serve. Many players have argued against this type of movement and refuse to do it. Their arguments are that it's too much work, and that when they follow this course, the other side always lobs over their heads. My replay to that is "bunk." If tennis is too much work, then you're not enjoying it—find another sport. Unless you're physically unable to move well, in which case play anyway you wish. There is no excuse for continually getting lobbed to death. If you move correctly, there is no reason one of you can't get to the lob. If you are getting lobbed to death, move your homebase at the net back a few steps making it easier to cover the lob.

The disadvantages to playing the one-up one-back formation are: your opponents have more court to hit into, there is less pressure on them, they have more angles to play with, and it is much easier to hit to the weaker players. Also, it is more boring. I'm sure you've seen a match where both teams play in this formation and the players at the baselines just keep hitting the ball back to each other. At the same time the players at the net fall asleep. This is an example of two singles games going on instead of a game of doubles.

Of course you will find yourself in this formation on occasion, in fact you start each point in this formation. I am saying that when the opportunity presents itself, get with your partner. Your ability level will also play a part in how soon you two can get together. It won't take the advanced players as long.

Remember, even in doubles it is impossible to cover the whole court. You can only cover *two-thirds* of the court, moving as a team you can cover the court better. If you move in the direction of the ball, it will be hard for your opponents to hit the open one-third of the court.

Lateral Movement

A. Both players are in their ready positions behind the baseline. B. As one player pulls wide to hit a forehand, his partner moves toward the middle of the court in anticipation of the next shot. These players know the "angles of probable return." C. Both players are in their ready positions at the net. D. As one player is pulled wide and up to hit a volley, her partner moves over to join her. He positions himself where the lines intersect at the service line in the middle, so that he is ready for either a volley or a lob. They both move toward the ball to cover the angles of probable return.

A

B

C

D

When playing doubles you sometimes find both teams in the 2-back or defensive formation. When this situation occurs, one type of strategic move you should try is to hit a dropshot and move into the net. You may think this is a good way to commit suicide. You are right unless you can get up to your homebase before your opponents get to the ball. If you can get there in time, your opponents will have to hit up on the ball, while you will be in position to hit down on the ball. You will only want to use this strategy once in a while to catch your opponents off guard. If your opponents don't move forward very well, you might want to use it more often.

In some cases you don't get to choose your own partner. When you do, you should look for a player who is, above all, easy going. And look for one who gives you positive encouragement and doesn't get upset when you miss a shot. You should prefer a player with about the same abilities as yours, that way your strategy should be the same.

All four players have key roles, and it is vital that you know your responsibilities if you are to be successful. The server's job is to get his *first* serve in. More points are lost on *second* serves than firsts. This goes for singles as well. Then, as soon as possible, join your partner at the net.

The server's partner's responsibilities are to put any returns that come his or her direction away. Also he should be active at the net even if he doesn't hit too many balls. That way your opponents will at least be thinking about you.

The returner's job is to get the ball back into play and at the same time keep it away from the opposing net person. A staggering figure that tennis statisticians came up with is that 25 percent of all returns are errors. You can see how important the return is. When returning, keep the ball as low as possible or put sufficient top spin on the ball so it will drop over the net quickly. Most players think that if their partner is returning serve, their job is not very important. Just the opposite is true, they are in a very critical position. It is their responsibility to call any faults that occur, thus taking that pressure off their partner so that he can totally concentrate on returning the serve. If the return goes past the net person, move up from your modified net position to your homebase at the net. If the ball doesn't make it that far, hold your position, be ready for anything, and hope for the best. If you see an overhead approaching, it might be wise to back up quickly and be prepared to defend yourself. For this reason the net position is comically referred to as the "hot box."

One common strategy used in singles and doubles is the serve and volley tactic. When you serve and volley in doubles there isn't as much pressure on you as in singles, since your partner is already at the net. When you approach, remember your split-step. You can either hit your first volley to the open court or right at the net person. I am not getting sadistic. You just aim the ball at your opponents' feet, making it difficult for them to handle the ball. That way you will keep your friends. Hitting into the open court will give you time to get to the net, while at the same time keeping the returner away from the net. This is the shot most preferred.

Lobbing the return of serve in doubles can be a very good tactic. Try to aim the lob over the net person's head, that way your opponents will have to switch sides of the court in order to cover it. Do this only on second serve, unless you have the utmost confidence in your lobs. The second serve will be easier to handle.

Poaching by the serving team is another effective strategy, though unfortunately it is not used enough. In order for a team to poach successfully, signals are needed. Do not spend hours devising complicated signals, such as baseball coaches use. Simple hand signals behind the back are sufficient. These signals can be any ones you want, just as long as both of you know what they are. Examples are using an open and closed fist, and using one and two fingers. I prefer using an open and closed fist because it is easier to see. If you are unsure of the signal have your partner repeat it before you serve. There is nothing more embarrassing than both players moving to the same side of the court while the ball is going to the other. As a poacher you should leave just before the returner makes contact with the ball. If you leave too early while he is still looking up, there will be plenty of time for him to adjust his return and hit behind you. Once you commit yourself, go all the way. Even if you don't get there in time it will still give the other team something to think about. When you are in the poach position picture yourself on first base ready to steal second. Just before contact move quickly.

The Australian formation is another good strategy to use once in a while. Use this formation sparingly in the ad court. The reasons for using this different formation are: it will minimize the angle of return of serve, and if your opponent has a great crosscourt return it will eliminate it. When this formation appears the returner has two choices: either a down-the-line return or a lob.

In the Australian formation the server stands right next to the center mark. After the serve, if he chooses to rush, he moves into position as if he were playing singles. His partner, meanwhile, is directly across the net from the opposing net person at his net position. The net person usually stays there, which is the purpose of this formation. However, to really mix things up try poaching from this position.

The "I" formation is another seldom used formation, though it can be very effective if used correctly. It can be used on either the deuce or ad side. Again the server starts out right next to the center mark, with his partner in an exaggerated crouched position in the center of the court near the net. Signals must be used with this formation to tell the server which way the net person will poach. After the server receives the signal he serves and rushes in toward his part-

160

Poaching

A. The player at the net gives his partner a signal so that he knows what he is going to do. B. The Server serves while his partner holds his position. C. As the server moves in, his partner holds position until the last possible second. D. As the receiver looks down to receive the serve, the net man moves over to pick off the opponent's return. E. The net man hits a winning volley, as his partner joins him at the net just in case it isn't a winner.

A

B

C

D

E

The Australian Formation

ner. Then just before the returner makes contact with the ball they split, each going in separate directions to cover the court.

How often have you seen this happen? A player with a weak serve, with his partner at the net, constantly having to fend for his life. Maybe you've been in this predicament yourself. As you know it's not much fun. So if you find yourself in this spot, instead of having a fuzz ball for brunch, make the smart move and go back and join your partner. Obviously this will put you on the defense, but it doesn't mean you have to stay there. As soon as you can, you want to gain the advantage at the net. From this formation there won't be as much pressure on the server.

So have fun with your doubles and try these different formations. They will make the game more interesting and they can help you win more matches.

Conditioning

TO ME, CONDITIONING means getting or keeping your body fit, in smooth working order. When you come off the court you may feel a little tired, but every muscle should not be sore. You should not be unable to play for a week because your muscles need time to recover.

I feel that almost everyone should be on some type of conditioning program. The program should be designed to fit the individual's specific needs and ability. In other words, you can choose from a variety of programs.

No matter what type of program you decide on or how extensive it is, it is important to be consistent with it. It is far better for you physically to do a specific program two to three times a week, than to do one real hard workout once a week. This is especially true for your heart.

The following are some ways to condition your body. These specific exercises will not only strengthen your body, but will also give you the confidence and endurance needed to finish a long match. How many times has this happened to you? Your match is tied one set a piece when all of a sudden your body tightens up, and it says to you, "lets quit!" And what do you usually do? Just what your body says. First you start going for outright winners that you know you can't possibly make, and finally you don't even try for some balls. Instead of calling them out, you call them "out of reach."

I know that feeling too well. You know you shouldn't do that, but you are too tired to do anything about it. Once you physically get tired, your mind is the next thing to go.

Tennis is only a partial conditioner, it can't do it all. So for those of you who only play once a week, conditioning is even more important.

Here are nine good reasons for conditioning:

1. It makes you feel better.
2. It helps you to relax.
3. It can improve your footwork.
4. It can help to improve your strokes.
5. It helps to make you mentally tough.
6. It will make it easier for you to recover between points.
7. It helps to prevent injuries that occur more easily when you get tired.
8. It helps to relieve tension.
9. It lets you be more patient and consistent during a rally.

Jumping Rope

THE SCHOOLYARD GAME OF jumping rope has become an art form, as well as a science. Boxers and basketball players have long known the benefits of jumping rope and now you can, too.

These benefits include:

1. Coordination.
2. Leg strength.
3. Endurance.
4. Stamina.
5. Foot quickness.

Jumping rope doesn't require a lot of time to get sufficient exercise. To help prevent injuries and make it more enjoyable, wear good quality tennis or jogging shoes and use a good quality jump rope.

Some experts say jumping rope for five minutes is equivalent to jogging two miles, though I feel it is closer to one mile.

Here are some techniques used in jumping rope:

1. Jump as if you are jogging.
2. Jump on one leg.
3. Jump on both legs simultaneously.

4. Boxer stop—alternate bouncing on one set of toes and heel and then alternate.
5. Crossovers—crossing your arms while jumping.
6. Double and tripple jump—twirling the rope two or three times between each jump.
7. Squat jumps—jumping rope from the squat position. Keep the knees extremely bent, while keeping the back straight. Make sure your knees are in fine shape before attempting this type of jump, because it is hard on the knees.
8. Jump rope backwards.

These four junior players are demonstrating four types of jump rope. From left to right, they are: jogging in place, squat jumps, crossovers, and the double-leg jump.

Flexibility Exercises

DUE TO THE UNNATURAL POSITIONS you find yourself in during play, it is extremely important to be flexible. Flexibility exercises, or stretching, is one of the best means of preventing injuries. Professional players already know the benefits of stretching. Because of their rigorous schedules it is a must. Some players use yoga, a form of flexibility exercises to stay loose and free of possible injury.

Stretching the muscles makes them more flexible and stronger, so you have a full range of motion. To get the full benefit from your flexibility exercises do them before and after you play. Stretching only takes five to ten minutes, though it seems we always have something better to do. These minutes can be the most important to your playing career, and can even lenghten your playing days. One caution however—do not bounce while stretching—bend slowly and smoothly. Bouncing will stretch the muscles too hard and fast. You might tear something. While stretching control your breathing by taking fairly deep breaths and letting them out slowly. This will help you to relax, which in turn makes it easier to stretch.

The benefits of flexibility exercises are many:

1. Relaxes the mind and body.
2. Causes freer and easier movement.
3. Tunes up the body.
4. Develops body awareness.
5. Promotes circulation.
6. Makes you feel good.
7. Helps prevent injuries.

Trunk or Body Twist

A. Start with your legs comfortably spread and arms extended at shoulder height.
B. Gently turn or twist the body to one side, Then the other. Repeat several times.
This is a fine flexibility exercise for the entire body.

A

B

This junior player is demonstrating the butterfly stretch. To do this flexibility exercise, sit on the court and bring your feet together as shown. Then slowly raise and lower your legs. This motion resembles the flapping action of a butterfly's wings. It is a good stretching exercise for your inner thigh muscles.

This is a demonstration of the basic hurdler's stretch. It resembles the body's position while sailing over a hurdle. Stretch out as this junior player has done and slowly slide your hands down the extended leg until you feel the muscles stretch. Do this several times, then repeat with the other leg. This is a fine flexibility exercise for all the muscles in the back of your legs.

Inverted Bicycle

Lie on your back, raise your legs, and place your hands under your hips for support. Move your legs as if you were pedaling a bicycle. Do this exercise for several minutes. It does not take the place of jogging, but it is a fine exercise for strengthening your lower back, legs, and stomach.

Toe Touches

Spread your legs comfortably apart and slide both arms down one leg until you feel the muscles stretch. Slide them back up and repeat stretch on the other leg. Do this exercise several times. It is good for stretching the legs and the back.

Back Stretch

Lie on your back with your legs extended. Slowly bring both legs over your head until they are resting on the floor. Try to bring your knees to the floor as shown in the illustration. This is a fine stretching exercise for all your back muscles.

Achilles Tendon Stretch

Start in a pushup position and raise up, arching your back. Rock slowly back until you feel the tendon stretching. Do this several times.

Back Arch

Lie on your back and slowly push up with your arms and legs until your back is arched. Hold the position for a second and then slowly lower yourself to the ground. Repeat several times. This exercise is designed for the back muscles, but you will also feel it in your arms and legs.

Strength Training

STRENGTH TRAINING HAS BEEN a sport throughout the ages. It hasn't been until recently that strength training has been recognized and given its due credit as a major contribution in the improvement of other sports. It is not enough to play yourself into shape any more.

Usually, when you think of strength training, you picture yourself as muscle-bound with less flexibility and less ability to move quickly. Contrary to this popular belief, strength training, if done properly, aids in:

1. Muscle tone—which you lose more easily as you get older.
2. Maintaining strength.
3. Prevention of injuries.
4. Rehabilitation after an injury.
5. Increasing strength.
6. Flexibility.
7. Increasing speed.
8. Adding more power to your strokes.

As far as juniors go and most adults, including women, strength training should be an essential part of an overall training program. Strength training is not just for body builders any more. If you have any doubts about your physical condition, check first with your physician and/or coach before engaging in any type of strength training program.

As with any other developmental program, you need to start out slowly and easily. If you have never had any previous experience in strength training it is important to learn how to do it correctly and safely. Either your local pro or a coach should be able to set up a good program that you can follow. Be sure to stay with this scheduled program long enough to give it a fair chance to show what it can do for you. Your program will probably consist of lifting weights twice a week, with two to three days' rest in between. Your lifting program should be done after your court workout, otherwise it will have a negative factor on your strokes. I recommend keeping a record of your strength training program. Chart your daily workouts so that you will have a good idea of how you are progressing.

Before you start lifting weights, be sure to do some flexibility exercises. This will loosen you up and help reduce possible injuries.

Be sure to always lift with someone else, preferrably someone with the same ability, not just for the safety factor, but also for motivation. As a safety factor you might consider the use of a weight belt, though there are two contradicting theories concerning its use. Some experts say it helps prevent back injuries, while others state that you rely too much on the other muscles, and so your back muscles don't develop enough. This will be one choice you have to make for yourself.

In the past the two basic forms of strength training have been with free weights or Universal strength training machines. These two methods are fine for strength training and many people prefer these styles. Free weight training has been in existence since the days of the early Greeks. Who knows, maybe the cave men even used a similar type of training to keep in shape for fighting dinosaurs. Free weights refers to lifting weight without the assistance of specially designed machines. This is the style of weight lifting we see on television that is used in all weight lifting competition. The advantage in using free weights is that they make it easier to build bulk or bigger muscles. Start out with light weights usually just ten to twenty pounds, depending on the specific muscle group you are working with. After you can handle seven repetitions fairly easily without much strain, then and only then, should you consider moving up to a higher weight.

Speaking to the men, myself included, we have a tendency to be too "macho" and try to lift too much too fast. This is where injuries can occur. Remember we are not lifting in order to look like Mr. Universe, but rather to be fit enough to last a long three or more set match .

The bars used are either solid steel or tubular steel, and the weights are either solid steel or plastic filled with sand. The starting price for an average set of weights is $30.00. If you want to include a weight bench the cost is at least another $35.00.

Universal circuit weight training systems have been on the market now for over twenty years. You can find these systems almost anywhere: in schools, colleges, YMCA's, and sports clubs, just to mention a few places. Due to the knowledge we have now about how physical fitness improves one's productivity, private businesses have even installed such systems within their facilities. These systems involve a series of resistance exercise machines that provide a vigorous workout for all major muscle groups. These systems or circuits can range anywhere from three to more than sixteen various machines. The machines should be set up so that you can work your way from one

Wrist Curls

Sit on the end of a weight bench or chair with your arm weight down. Slowly raise and lower the weight, trying to keep the forearm flat on the bench and only moving the wrist and the hand. This will strengthen your wrist and forearm muscles.

Bench Press

Lie on a bench with your feet comfortably spread apart and your back flat against the bench. Lift the bar off the supports with your hands about shoulder width apart. Slowly bring the bar down to just above the nipples on your chest; press it back up until your arms are almost straight. This is a fine exercise for developing and strengthening your shoulders, arms, and chest.

machine to the next, right around the room. If the system is set up properly two consecutive machines won't work on the same muscle group. This is important because muscle fibers need a chance to recover between lifts, otherwise they will become overtaxed. Start out with a particular weight with which you can do seven repetitions without stress. To get a good workout, it is recommended that you complete the full circuit three to five times. This means using each particular machine anywhere from 21 to 35 times. This will probably be too much for most of you at first, but it will give you a goal to strive for. This type of program will cost the individual anywhere from one thousand to many thousands of dollars.

Position yourself under the shoulder pads of the Universal machine and hold onto the bar. You will be in the crouch position. Slowly almost straighten your legs, keeping your back straight. Lower the weight until it is completely down. This is a great strengthening exercise for your legs, buttocks, and stomach, and lower back.

Leg curl or extension demonstrated on a Universal strength training machine. Sit on the machine with your back against the back support, legs wrapped through the extension section. Start with your legs down; lift them until they are parallel to the floor; slowly lower them. This is a good exercise for your quadriceps (upper rear leg muscles).

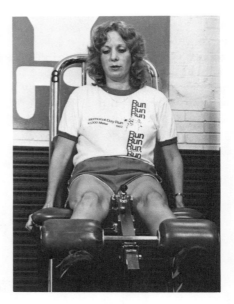

Leg press demonstrated on a Universal strength training machine. Sit on the machine with your back firmly pressed against the upper portion of the seat, legs bent and close to chest. Slowly press the legs forward until they are almost straight, then slowly bring the legs back toward your chest. This is a good exercise for your buttocks, quadriceps, and hamstrings.

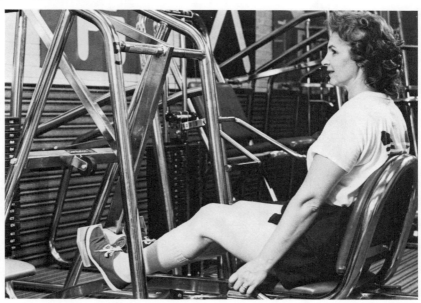

A strength training chapter would not be complete without a section devoted to "Nautilus" training. These various machines work on a system of cams and pulleys designed to give the user a full range of motion. The name "Nautilus" comes from the nautilus sea shells, which are the shape of the cams. This relatively new training method has been on the market since 1971. Nautilus machines are the only machines that provide you with a full range of exercise. In order to give a full range of exercise a system first must fit these ten requirements.*

1. Positive work.
2. Negative work.
3. Balanced resistance.
4. Rotary movement.
5. Direct resistance.
6. Variable resistance.
7. Prestretching.
8. Unrestricted speed of movement.
9. Stretching.
10. Resistance at the point of full muscle contraction.

However, these machines will only provide you with a full range of exercise if done properly. By properly I mean using the proper techniques involved with each machine. Proper style or technique is a must before you can improve to your potential. Each machine works on a specific muscle group. Your usual routine starts out by checking your weight and normal pulse rate. Next you do some flexibility exercises to loosen up your muscles. Then it is off to the stationary bicycle for a few minutes of cardiovascular work. The time spent cycling will vary according to your present condition.

Next you start with the specific Nautilus machines, first working on the larger muscle groups of the legs and proceding down to the smaller muscle groups of the arms. To get the most out of each exercise, bring the weight up using a two count and then a four count to return the weight. This way you are putting emphasis on the negative resistance aspect that you will find is harder to do. Also, be sure to contract or flex your muscles when the weight is most resistant. This will cause your muscles to work even harder.

After the last machine, it is time for some sit-ups on an inclined board. For your final work-out, go back to the stationary bicycle.

*Source: *How Your Muscles Work*, Ellington Darden, Ph.D., Anna Publishing Inc., Winter Park, FL. 32793, p. 8.

Immediately after you finish your bike work-out, you are required to check your "active" pulse rate. You then check a chart to see if your pulse rate is where it should be. It is also a good indication of the intensity of your training session.

There may be anywhere from fifteen to thirty various exercises you can do at the center. Depending on intensity, your workout can last anywhere from twenty minutes to one hour.

Throughout your whole program, if your center is like the one here in Cedar Rapids, Iowa, you will be under the watchful eyes of highly qualified instructors. You will find them very safety conscious and genuinely interested in your progress.

The best part of your workout comes in the form of a hot tub, after you have completed your work out. If you haven't experienced one before, you will be amazed at how effective it is in relieving sore and tired muscles. Be sure to stay in just a few minutes, any longer and you may come out too weak.

There are over six hundred Nautilus Centers located throughout the United States with each one having basically the same equipment, format, and qualified instruction. I would recommend that you try out one of these centers. It might just be what you need.

Nautilus Machines

These are only four of the many types of Nautilus machines available. A. Hip and back machine—develops and strengthens the muscles of the buttocks, hips, and lower back regions. B. Pullover machine—develops and strengthens the muscles of the shoulders and back. C. Torso-arm machine—develops and strengthens the muscles of the shoulders and back. D. Double chest machine—develops and strengthens muscles of the upper and lower chest.

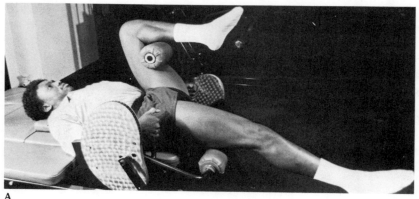

A

B

D

C

Isometric exercises are another fine means to get into playing condition. Isometric means pushing against a fixed object such as a wall.

Isometrics—Wall Press

The idea of this strength training exercise is to stand beside a wall and simply press your racquet against the wall. The harder you press, the better the exercise works. You can do this exercise for all your basic strokes. This strength training exercise develops and strengthens the muscles of the wrist and forearms.

Isometrics—Hand Press and Hand Pull

A. Press your hands together. B. Try to pull your hands apart. Both exercises help to develop and strengthen wrists and forearms.

A

B

Any of these strength training programs would be an adequate means of improving your tennis game. You may even want to combine two types in order to fit your specific needs. Whatever method you choose, stay with it. You will be amazed at how much it will improve your game.

I hate to admit it, but strength training is not one of my favorite activities, so if you are like me you might need to be pressured or forced into strength training. The best way I have found to do this is by joining a YMCA, Nautilus Center, or some other fitness center. Since you have already spent money to join, you don't want to waste your hard-earned money by not using the facility. If you truly want to be on a program and can't get self-motivated, try one of these programs and get into shape.

The author and his son Matthew demonstrating a strength training exercise called "child lifts." This is one way to become a closer-knit family while strengthening your leg and stomach muscles.

Rope Twist

Hold your arms out straight, parallel to the ground. Turn the bar in your hands, slowly bringing the weight up to the bar.

Chin-ups or Pull-ups

Hang on to a bar with your arms extended and pull yourself up slowly. You can install a bar in any door opening. This is a great exercise for strengthening shoulders, upper back, and chest.

This junior player is demonstrating cover power. With your racquet cover on your racquet, practice all your strokes as you would in mirror tennis. You can even practice your footwork. For added weight you can put a book or something else that is fairly lightweight in your cover. This exercise will strengthen the muscles of your shoulders, forearms, wrists, and hands.

Wall Pushups

This is one of the most demanding of the strength training exercises. It would be advisable to take your shoes off so that you don't mar the wall, and you may want to place a pillow under your head. Stand two feet from the wall and go into a handstand with your feet against the wall. Press up into a handstand until your arms are straight. Do as many of these as you can. This is a difficult, but excellent, exercise for strengthening your shoulders, fore- arms, neck, chest, wrists, hands, and stomach.

Leg-raises

Lie on your back with your arms at your sides. Lift your legs six inches off the ground and hold them for several seconds. Slowly lower the legs and repeat. Do not rest between leg-raises. This will strengthen your lower back, leg, and stomach muscles.

Pushups

Lie face down with your arms shoulder width apart, placed on either side of your chest. Slowly push down, raising your body and legs off the floor. Keep your back parallel to the floor. Slowly lower your body until your chest just touches the floor. This is a basic strength training exercise that is good for your shoulders, arms, chest, and lateral back muscles.

This junior player is demonstrating the basic exercise of sit-ups. Lie on your back with your legs bent. Lock your hands behind your head and slowly sit up until your elbows touch your knees. Then lower your upper body until your back (but not your head) touches the floor. Repeat the exercise several times, gradually doing more as you gain strength. Instead of placing your hands behind your head, you may cross them over your chest. It is important to keep your chin tucked down while doing this exercise. Sit-ups are an excellent method of strengthening the stomach and back muscles.

This junior player is in midair demonstrating the kangaroo hop. The object is to jump as high as you can while bringing your knees up to your chest. It is an excellent way to strengthen your leg muscles and is also good for controlling your emotions.

Sprints

SPRINTING IS ANOTHER supplementary training exercise which, if done regularly, can improve your game. In tennis you don't run long distances, you run many short races against the ball. Professional players have recently become aware of the importance of good sprinting technique. This can be seen in the number of players turning to such men as Henry Hines, former world class sprinter turned sprinting coach.

Sprinting technique varies from your jogging technique in that you run on the balls of your feet as opposed to running more or less flat-footed. For additional speed pump your arms vigorously.

Sprint practice can be done anywhere including the court. Two ways to practice on the court are: running the lines and the sixty-second drill. Running the lines is similar to the drill used in basketball. This drill involves running from the baseline to the service line, back to the baseline, then up to the net, and finally back to the baseline. If this isn't enough for you, try the sixty-second drill. In this drill you first place a ball every place where two lines intersect on the court. There will be eleven balls on the court. You have sixty seconds to pick up all the balls and put them in a basket.

Running up and down hills and running up steps are two more ways for developing leg strength and quickness. If you try these methods, be careful not to go too fast and end up going out of control. It is possible to get hurt using these techniques. If sprinting is part of your overall program it should be done at least three times a week.

Walking, hiking, swimming, and bicycling are all means of developing leg strength.

Plyometric Training

IF YOU ARE LOOKING FOR YET one more form of supplementary training give Plyometrics a try. I personally have been using this technique for a couple of years, never knowing what it was called or its true value. Plyometrics—hopping and bouncing drills—first came to our American coaches' attention at the 1972 Summer Olympics in Munich. Russian and East German coaches had been using this training technique for years in training their sprinters. Plyometrics will do more to increase your speed, quickness, and general conditioning than even uphill runs or downhill runs. Plyometrics is advantageous in that it can be practiced indoors or out. If practiced indoors, be sure to do it on mats, wear good quality shoes, and, if necessary, heel-cups to avoid undo stress on your feet and legs.

There are two basic types of plyometrics: power bounds and speed hops. Power bounds consist of jumping as high and far as possible. Speed hops involve hopping as fast as possible to a predetermined distance. With either method you can either bound or hop on one foot or both feet.

If you attempt this type of training, be prepared for a very rigorous workout. You will probably find it the single hardest type of workout in your life, but it will be well worth the effort. It should be done at least three times a week if you want to improve.

Jogging

JOGGING, IF DONE PROPERLY, will improve one's physical condition as well as his tennis game. However, jogging is definitely not for everyone, so don't feel it's a requirement for better tennis. It's just one of many supplementary exercise plans that will help to improve your endurance, leg muscle development, balance, speed, and flexibility needed to sustain a long match. Jogging can even help you lose weight, and has been known to help take inches off your hips and other areas of the body.

If you decide jogging might be for you and you are unsure of your physical condition, or if you are over thirty years old, you should consult with a physician before starting. A thorough examination is a good idea before undertaking any form of strenuous exercise especially if you are overweight, have a tendency to have high blood pressure, or if your family has a history of heart disease. Some doctors recommend that everyone over 40 have a stress test.

As with any form of excercise, be sure to stretch first to loosen up your muscles. If possible jog with a friend or friends. The companionship will help pass the time, provide encouragement, and be a source of protection. Jogging, like everything else, is mainly mental stress in that you are competing against yourself. This is where a companion really comes in handy.

At first just walk a mile or two. If you feel no discomfort, such as chest pains or dizziness, jog easily for thirty seconds. If you still feel fine, you should be ready to start jogging. Start out jogging slowly and easily, you are not out to set any speed records. Jog and walk until you work up a sweat, or until your legs begin to get tired. Two to three minutes may be enough at first. Gradually you can build up to one to two miles or ten to twenty minutes. This is enough distance to jog for tennis since you are not in marathon training. The most common mistake beginning joggers make is to try to do too much too fast. The only thing that does for you is to make you sore, and you lose your enthusiasm for jogging.

If you're like me you dread the thought of jogging in the bitter cold of winter. But as I have found out, winter jogging can be tolerated and can even be enjoyable if you learn to dress properly. If you dress with too many layers of clothes you will get overheated quickly. If you dress too lightly, your body will get chilled too quickly. Experience is the best key to how much to wear. Everyone has a different tolerance for cold weather. I would suggest wearing a warm layer, then a tee shirt that will trap the warm air next to your body, and then add a layer of wool. Wool is the only material that will hold the heat in even when it gets wet. For extremely cold temperatures additional layers may be needed. Wear a pair of wool socks for the same reason. A hat and gloves are also recommended in cold weather. Remember 40 percent of your body heat is lost through the head.

During the winter your jogging distance may need to be altered slightly at first, to compensate for the change in climate and additional layers of clothing. Once your body gets used to this new experience you can increase your milage back to normal.

You may also decide to change your route during these months. It may be advisable to stay a little closer to home in case some unforeseen obstacle arises. If the sidewalks or roads get too slippery or icy, I would recommend another form of exercise. It is too easy to slip and get hurt, and we don't want that to happen.

You may even want to try jogging in your local gymnasium, or YMCA. If you live near a college, you might inquire about using their facilities. In most cases you will find these facilities willing to help you out, though you may have to pay a small fee.

Remember jogging should be fun, not a chore.

Your Pulse Rate

BEFORE AND AFTER JOGGING, or for that matter any form of physical activity, it is advisable to monitor your heart beat by taking your pulse. To find your pulse hold your first two fingers on the lower part of your wrist or on your neck. To calculate your active pulse rate, record it for ten seconds, then multiply that number times six to find it for the minute. Below is a pulse rate guide for you to go by.

YOUR PULSE RATE GUIDE*

Women

Age	Min	Opt	Max
25	130	157	185
30	126	153	180
35	123	149	175
40	119	145	170
45	116	140	165
50	112	136	160
55	109	132	155
60	105	128	150
65	102	123	145

* Taken from *The Complete Book of Running* by James F. Fixx, Random House, Inc. P. 68.

Men

Age	Min	Opt	Max
25	137	166	195
30	133	162	190
35	130	157	185
40	126	153	180
45	123	149	175
50	119	145	170
55	116	140	165
60	112	136	160
65	109	132	155

If you undertake jogging you need to be aware of the most common injuries that may occur. As with any other injuries, prevention is the key. You can prevent most injuries by:

1. Doing flexibility exercises before and after jogging.
2. Wearing proper shoes, ones that are flexible. Average cost about $30–$40.
3. Running easily and stopping when it hurts.
4. Resting aching legs.
5. Dressing according to the weather.
6. Using your normal stride.
7. Letting your arms do some of the work. Too often I see joggers running with their arms at their sides. I recommend using your arms in a pumping action. It will make it easier to sustain your pace and make less work for your legs.
8. Avoid running on your toes.
9. Warming down after jogging.
10. Wearing bright clothes when running at night.
11. Jogging in well-lighted areas.
12. Jogging in familiar areas.
13. Avoiding always jogging on hard surfaces.
14. Not jogging outside when it's icy.

Runner's Injuries

I AM GOING TO LIST only some of the injuries that are possible from jogging. Don't let them scare you off though! You may never get an injury and in most cases if you do, it won't be serious. I just want to prepare you for what can happen. My suggestions are only suggestions. Since I am not allowed to practice medicine I have listed only a few of the causes, *home treatments*, and preventions of these injuries. With any injury that you think might be serious, don't hesitate to contact a physician. If you are worried about injuries, or just interested in them, I would suggest purchasing one of the many fine sports medicine books on the market.

1. Runner's knee. Forty percent of all runner's injuries happen to the knees. Simply speaking, the kneecap rubs the wrong way, creating a softening of the cartilage around the knee. Symptoms of runner's knee are: pain, stiffness, and swelling. Home treatment for this injury consists of rest, cutting down on mileage, and strengthening exercises.
2. Blisters. See Chapter on Tennis Injuries.
3. Heat stroke. See Chapter on Tennis Injuries.
4. Cramps. A cramp is a painful, prolonged contraction of the fibers in a muscle, caused by strain. It can last anywhere from a few seconds to several hours. One cause of cramps can be lack of salt. If you get a cramp you can relieve the pain by stretching, kneading the muscle, and walking. If cramps occur I would suggest not running anymore that day.
5. Ankle problems. See Chapter on Tennis Injuries.
6. Stitches. Stitches is a form of a cramp on the side. It is a sudden, sharp pain in the upper part of the abdomen, the stomach region. Severity of pain varies with different joggers. A main cause is eating just before jogging. If stitches occur walk until pain subsides. It is usually best not to jog anymore that day.
7. Muscle soreness. Muscle soreness is due to overuse of the muscles. The best treatment here is prevention. Know your

limitations and don't overdo it. When this injury does occur all you can really do is rest. In most cases a couple of days will be enough. Then resume jogging, however, shorten your mileage until you are in better condition. Your body should tell you when you can increase your mileage, so listen to it!

8. Shin splints. Shin splints is a pain in the back or front of the lower part of the leg. It is usually caused by jogging on hard surfaces. It can also be caused by jogging too high on the toes, and from shoes that are too stiff. Rest, along with jogging on grass, is the best treatment.

9. Bone bruises. Bone bruises usually occur to the heels. Again this is due to jogging on hard surfaces. Rest and jogging on grass is the best treatment. Heel cups or pads can be purchased to keep the injury from getting worse. If any injury persists, consult your physician immediately. You don't want it to get worse.

10. Loss of a toenail. This may not be one of your more severe injuries, but it is fairly common, and it can be annoying, if not downright painful. It is caused by constant rubbing against the inside of your shoe. It can also be caused by shoes that are too small. This injury can also occur while playing tennis, for the same reasons, though in tennis it can also occur if you have a habit of dragging your toes. If this injury happens to you, cover the area with a protective pad while jogging or playing. In addition, let it air out as much as possible.

11. Heel bruise. This condition is an inflamation of the heel. It is usually caused by running on a hard surface. Wearing a good pair of shoes should help to eliminate this type of injury. If it occurs, you may have to curtail your running for a while until the pain subsides. Then start out slowly again on a softer surface, such as a track. Placing heel cups in your shoes will help to relieve some of the pain.

12. Even though winter jogging can be fun, you should also be aware of two possible dangers. They are frostbite and hypothermia. Frostbite occurs to your extremities—ears, fingers, toes, and face. The symptoms of frostbite are numbness, swelling, and a whitening of the affected area. If this happens to you, stop jogging immediately. Place the exposed area in *warm* water 100°–110° only. Any other home treatment could make the situation worse. Consult your physician as soon as possible.

195

13. Hypothermia, on the other hand, refers to being subjected to the harsh winter elements for a prolonged period of time. People who have been lost in the wilderness for days or boaters who have been thrown into cold water suffer from this. It should never happen to a smart jogger. As previously mentioned, during the winter you should alter your jogging course to more populated areas, and jog with a friend. As the old saying goes "let your common sense be your guide." I guess that was conscience, but it still applies. If, for some unforeseen reason, you get hypothermia, get warm and dry as soon as possible, and consult your physician immediately.

Tennis Injuries

AS MENTIONED IN THE introduction I'm an advocate of preventive medicine, which to me means doing everything possible to prevent a possible injury from occurring. The reason is that I hate pain! I'm sure quite a few of you feel the same way. So what do we do? We usually don't give it a second thought. We think an injury won't happen to us, and this is when they occur. Here are some ways of preventing injuries:

1. Being on a daily flexibility program.
2. Strength training to keep your muscles in tone.
3. Easy jogging for cardiovascular conditioning.
4. Using proper equipment, *i.e.*, shoes, correct size racquet, and so forth.
5. Jumping rope, also good for cardiovascular conditioning.
6. Warming up properly by giving your body time to get loosened up before you engage in strenuous exercise.
7. Knowing when to stop before you get overfatigued.
8. Having regular checkups by your physician, usually once a year, more often if your condition warrants it.
9. Make sure you start out with qualified instruction. There are professionals who can put you on the proper program and correct any flaws in your strokes that can lead to problems.

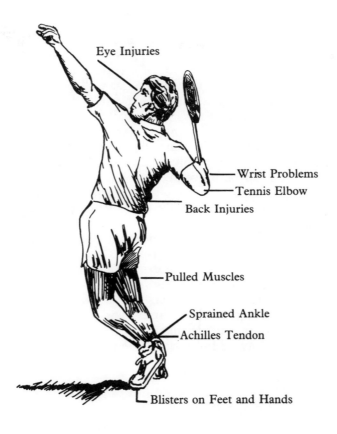

Eye Injuries

Wrist Problems

Tennis Elbow

Back Injuries

Pulled Muscles

Sprained Ankle

Achilles Tendon

Blisters on Feet and Hands

Even after taking these preventive steps, injuries unfortunately can and will occur. It is up to us to deal with them the best we can. Since we all have different thresholds of pain, injuries will affect each of us differently.

The following are some of the most common injuries related to tennis.

197

Blisters

A blister is caused by heat and is a localized collection of fluid between the first and second layers of skin. Within this pocket the liquid can be in the form of pus, blood, or serum.

Blisters can occur on your feet as well as your hands. In the case of your hands, they usually occur when the racquet turns in your hand. With your feet they are usually caused by repeated stopping and turning sharply. Wearing a new pair of shoes can also cause them. Even though they are not usually serious, they can be very painful, and if neglected, can result in serious infections and complications.

Blisters can be prevented by:

1. Using powder in your socks while playing.
2. Wearing two pairs of socks.
3. Wearing the tennis shoes that best fit your feet.
4. Using resin on your grip.
5. Doing strengthening exercises for your grip.
6. Having the proper grip size.
7. Not playing when your feet or hands start hurting.
8. Watching the ball closely and trying to hit the ball in the center of your strings.
9. Not playing for a long time in a new pair of shoes.

Your home treatment will involve:

1. Stop playing immediately after one starts hurting. If this is not possible cover with a protective bandage.
2. If you can catch one just as it is beginning to form, stop playing and apply a relatively new product called "New-Skin." When this liquid is applied directly over the blister it can help prevent it from getting worse.
3. You can either let it break on its own, or lance it yourself with a sterilized needle. If you decide to lance it, let the old skin protect it while the new inner layer is forming, and cover it with a bandaid. If the old skin is completely separated place a pad, such as moleskin, cut slightly larger than the blister, over the blister to cushion it. Cut a hole big enough to expose the blister so that it can air. However, if you are a diabetic, consult your physician first before administering this home treatment.

4. If there is extreme pain don't play for a few days, but do some supplemental training exercises.

Blisters have been known to result in blood poisioning, so do not take them lightly.

Sprains

A sprain is a partial or complete tearing of one or more ligaments (bands of tough tissue) that surround a joint, due to forcing the joint beyond its normal range of motion. It usually happens to an ankle, though it can also occur to wrists, elbows, and shoulders. Sprains can be very painful, and if left untreated can become serious. Sprains can be categorized into three degrees. The first degree consists of mild disability. The second degree consists of a prolonged pain, and the third degree consists of severe pain and loss of motion. Whenever a sprain is of the second or third degree nature, consult a physician.

Sprains are commonly caused by:

1. Turning or stopping too sharply.
2. Stepping on a loose ball.
3. Stepping off the court, if it is a raised one.
4. Falling and landing on your wrist.
5. Unusual stress from improper contact with the ball.
6. Freak accidents.

You can help prevent sprains from occurring by:

1. Being on a strength program and strengthening the muscles in your ankles, wrists, elbows, and shoulders.
2. Keeping stray balls off the court.
3. Not trying for balls that are out or out of reach.
4. Not wearing shoes that are too large for your feet.

Home treatments for sprains include:

1. Immediately after one occurs elevate the injured part slightly above the level of your heart. Apply ice on and off for at least 24 hours to reduce swelling and to prevent further complications. When applying ice to any injury it is advisable to place a towel between the ice and the skin to prevent irritations.

2. Stay off the injury as much as possible.
3. Once the swelling has subsided, heat or a combination of heat and ice can be applied to generate more circulation and to allow the optimum healing processes to occur.
4. Once healing has begun, slowly start your flexibility and strength training program to rebuild and strengthen the injured area.
5. Ankle braces and elastic bandages are available that help provide minimal support to the injured area.

Strained or pulled muscles

strained or pulled muscle occurs when a few fibers are torn away om the muscle. A more severe form occurs when there is a complete ıpture of a muscle. When minor strains occur there will be pain, ıssibly severe, limitation of motion, and weakness of the muscle.

This injury is commonly caused by:

1. Overextending for a ball.
2. Muscle fatigue.
3. Not taking 5 to 10 minutes or more, depending on your condition, to warm up.
4. Lack of skill.
5. Trying to do too much for your physical condition.

These pulled muscles can be prevented by:

1. Warming up slowly.
2. Being on flexibility, strength training, and jogging programs.
3. Not over exerting oneself to the point of exhaustion.
4. Developing the skills needed for tennis.

Home treatments for this type of injury are:

1. When a pulled muscle occurs, immediately apply ice for at least 30 minutes. Then keep applying it on and off for 24 hours, while keeping the injured muscle elevated.
2. Stay off the injured limb, and allow it time to rest.
3. When the pain subsides, start your flexibility, strength training, and jogging programs to strengthen your muscles.

Back injuries

Back injuries or backaches usually occur in the lower back area. They are not usually severe, though they can be, but they are irritating. These back problems are generally because of a pulled muscle. These injuries are caused by improper serving technique or playing too much for your ability level.

Prevention of back injuries includes:

1. Being on a flexibility and strength training program.
2. Avoiding the American Twist serve, which causes you to arch your back in an unnatural position.
3. Warming up your serve well before serving hard.
4. Not practicing your serve or overhead for a prolonged period of time.

Home treatments for back injuries are:

1. Stop playing immediately after you feel some pain in your back, so a more severe pain won't occur.
2. Apply heat to the injured area of the back. Heat will help relieve the pain. If that does not help some physicians suggest using ice for the first twelve hours, then using heat the second day or until pain subsides.
3. Get a nice back massage from your spouse or friend.
4. Rest the injured muscles until the pain subsides. If pain persists consult your physician.
5. If the injury is believed to be severe, immediately consult your physician. This, of course, is true for any injury.
6. When you resume play, take it easy at first.
7. If you aren't already on one, begin a flexibility and strength training program after the injury has healed.

Heat stroke

This serious fast-acting physical condition is caused by the inability of the temperature-regulating cells in the brain to increase the body's mechanism of removing heat. This causes a sudden, uncontrollable rise in body temperature. Heat stroke is liable to happen when the temperature and humidity are high.

A player suffering from heat stroke may show signs of:

1. Being unconscious.
2. Having a very rapid pulse rate.
3. Having hot flushed skin.
4. Running a very high fever.

Prevention of heat stroke includes:

1. Avoiding playing at the hottest part of the day.
2. Drinking plenty of liquids during play so that you don't get dehydrated.
3. Taking frequent breaks in the shade.
4. Wearing a hat to protect your head and neck.
5. Wearing white clothes that reflect the heat.
6. Wearing loose clothes so that the heat can escape.

There is no home treatment for heat stroke. Immediately after this condition has been diagnosed, either call an ambulance to transport the victim, or drive him to the hospital yourself. This is one injury you don't want to take a chance with. While waiting for an ambulance, keep the victim lying down with legs elevated above the level of the heart to get blood back to the brain.

Heat exhaustion

Heat exhaustion is a much slower acting condition than heat stroke and can take several days before you start feeling its effect. During the first few days you will feel more tired and weaker than normal.

This condition is brought on by severe dehydration and loss of salt in the body.

Signs that heat exhaustion may be present are:

1. Fatigue.
2. Abdominal pain.
3. Cramps.
4. Nausea.
5. Skin may be moist and pale.

Heat exhaustion can be prevented if you take the same recommended safety procedures that you use against heat stroke.

Treatment for heat exhaustion consists of replenishing the liquids (fruit juices are good), and salts the body requires. Stop playing for the day. As soon as the signs occur, immediately consult a physician. If left untreated, shock can result.

Eye injuries

Eye injuries are very painful and can be serious. Since your eyesight is so important, extreme care should be taken. Obviously eye injuries are caused by being struck in or around the eye, usually with the ball. Before striking the eye the ball most frequently comes off your opponent's racquet, though occasionally the ball may come off your racquet. After being struck in the eye you will generally notice immediate pain, swelling, and discoloration—black and blue.

Suggested precautions for prevention of eye injuries are:

1. While playing doubles don't look back to see what your partner is doing, or where the ball is.
2. Don't play so close to the net that you don't have sufficient time to react.
3. Use proper stroking techniques.
4. Wear protective eye glasses.
5. Concentrate on the ball.
6. Keep the ball away from your body.

Home treatment for eye injuries include:

1. Stop playing and immediately apply ice to reduce swelling and to prevent further damage. Be careful not to leave ice on too long due to the sensitivity of the area.
2. Don't take any chances. Consult your physician.

Achilles tendon injuries

The Achilles tendon, if injured, can be a severe and crippling ailment. The injury occurs when the tendon is torn away from its attachment either partially or completely. When a tear occurs you will know immediately. You hear a distinct popping sound, feel sudden pain, and lose the function of that limb.

This type of injury is caused by sharp, sudden movements as when you start after a ball, or by sprinting hard while up on your toes.

203

This possible crippling injury can be prevented by:

1. Resting sore and tired legs.
2. Running hills to strengthen the legs.
3. Doing flexibility exercises before you play.
4. Being on strength training, jogging, and sprinting programs.
5. Warming up properly before playing hard.

Treatment will depend on the severity of the injury, though your physician should be consulted immediately, in any case.

If the injury is mild the treatment involves:

1. Applying ice.
2. Elevating the leg.
3. Compression.
4. Staying off the leg by using crutches.

When you get your doctor's permission you can:

1. Use whirlpool baths.
2. Hot compresses.
3. A mild massage.

All three treatments will aid in circulation, since tendons generally have poor circulation. When pain subsides start your mild exercise programs.

Wrist injuries

Unless it is a sprain or you fracture it by falling, wrist injuries are not too serious, just painful and irritating.

The causes of wrist injuries are numerous. They are:

1. Using a racquet that is too heavy for you.
2. Using an improper grip size.
3. Not watching the ball close enough.
4. Mis-hits.
5. Hitting the ball late.
6. Serving too hard.
7. The racquet turning in your hand.
8. Weak wrists.

Prevention of wrist injuries are:

1. Making sure you have the proper size racquet.
2. Using proper stroking mechanics.
3. Watching the ball carefully.
4. Being on a strength training program.

Home treatment for this injury involves:

1. Lessons to correct faulty strokes.
2. Rest arm until pain subsides.
3. Hot compresses.
4. Mild massage.
5. Flexibility and strength training programs.

Tennis elbow

Tennis elbow is not the most common, but is the best known, and at the same time, the least understood of all tennis injuries. If not detected early it can develop into an injury so bad it can retard your playing activities or halt them permanently. It can occur on either the inner or outer side of the elbow. This most discussed injury is due to excessive strain on the muscles of the forearm that attach to the elbow, usually below the elbow joint. The inflamed area can even be a result of small tears to these muscles. You would be surprised at how many cases of tennis elbow are not even caused from playing tennis. Besides carpentry, other causes can be: fishing, baseball, and being an electrician, just to mention a few. No matter what the cause, the elbow is prone to injury since it has a tendency to absorb shock.

Early symptoms of tennis elbow are pain and difficulty in lifting a glass of water, opening a door, shaking hands, or any other minor action that we take for granted.

It is a shame to see players with this injury or about ready to get it, and know they can do something to cure it or prevent it from occurring. At the same time it makes me sick seeing pro shops stocked with elbow supports. It makes me wonder what pros are doing to help cure this major tennis problem, or are they just taking advantage of it?

I, for one, have suffered from tennis elbow for over a year. After all kinds of various treatments, I ended up having surgery as a last resort. The surgery has been successful, though I am still on a re-

205

Ouch! I bet that hurt! This man demonstrates what a player looks like when he leads with his elbow. Remember, that elbow support isn't on his arm for looks!

habilitation program, consisting of strength training. I do know how it feels, and I can sympathize with those of you who have suffered from it, too. However, I should explain that my injury was not due to tennis, but rather from being a carpenter.

Whenever a teaching pro sees signs of this injury, he should make it his priority to rid that person of this potentially painful and crippling injury.

The common causes of tennis elbow are:

1. A weak forearm.
2. Your thumb extended up the back of the grip on the backhand, which usually makes you push through the stroke from the elbow.
3. Leading with the elbow on the backhand and forehand.
4. Hitting the ball late.
5. Hitting the ball too far away from the body.
6. Using an improper grip such as an eastern forehand or western.
7. Using a racquet that is too heavy for you.
8. Using a racquet that is either too flexible or too stiff for you.
9. Playing for longer periods of time than your body can take.
10. Serving while using the "frying-pan" grip.
11. Lack of follow-through.
12. Flipping the wrist for added top spin.
13. Playing on fast surfaces.
14. Using heavy balls.
15. Having your racquet strung too tight for your strength.
16. Hitting the ball too close to the body.
17. Using the American Twist serve.

This major tennis problem can be prevented by:

1. Being on flexibility and strength training programs.
2. Using proper stroking techniques.
3. Resting the elbow if it gets sore.
4. Using the correct size and weight racquet.
5. Keeping the elbow warm before play.

Home treatment for tennis elbow will vary with the severity of the injury. Such treatments include:

1. Resting the injured elbow until pain subsides.
2. Taking lessons to improve your strokes. When you make contact with the ball your muscles will be contracted with the elbow slightly bent or straight. You should never hit the ball with an extremely bent elbow. It is also very important to meet the ball in *front* of your body.
3. After healing has taken place, slowly begin flexibility and strength training programs.

4. With milder cases use heat treatments, massage, and whirl-pool baths.
5. Use ice compacts after playing for no longer than 20 minutes to reduce swelling.
6. Use the correct grips.
7. If you have to use an elbow support, make sure it is not too tight and that it is reasonably wide.
8. I have heard some cases of players changing hands. If they are right-handed, they play left. This is only recommended in unusual cases. Most players have enough trouble playing with their dominant hand. If that's your only option, give it a try.
9. Don't serve quite so hard.
10. Serve underhand.
11. Use a two-handed backhand. That will take the strain off the elbow.
12. If pain persists consult your physician.

Racquets

TENNIS RACQUETS HAVE CHANGED dramatically since the sport originated. When the sport began it resembled handball. Hands were used in place of racquets. Later, crude racquets were fashioned out of wood, covered with parchment. These early racquets were of various shapes.

If you are either just starting out or an experienced veteran, choosing the correct racquet will be one of the most important decisions you will make in your tennis career. The most important aspect in choosing a racquet is that it should feel comfortable in your hand. It should feel like an extension of your arm rather than a foreign object. The better the racquet feels to you, the more confidence you will have, and the better you will play. Racquet preference is purely personal, so pick the one suited for you. It doesn't matter if it is not the most popular model or the one your friends use.

When considering a racquet, keep these points in mind.

1. Your ability.
2. How often you play.

3. Your grip size.
4. What type of racquet you are interested in.
5. The specific characteristics of a racquet—weight, balance, and flexibility.
6. Type of strings.
7. Size of the racquet.
8. Price range.

As you see there are a lot of things to consider in deciding on a racquet.

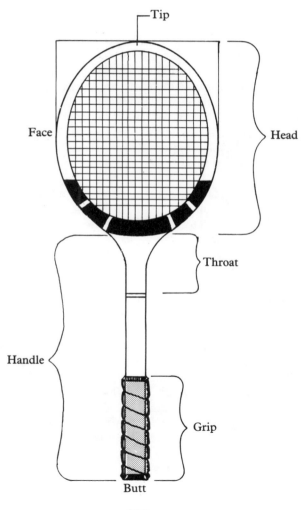

According to the tennis rules, there are no specifications governing the size and shape of racquets. Racquets range in size from mini to oversized with junior, regular, and mid or medium size racquets in between. Mini racquets are the group of racquets classified by the "Graduated Length Method." These wood racquets range from 6 to 3 inches shorter than regular racquets. Junior racquets come in both wood and metal. They are 2 inches shorter than regular racquets. Midsize racquets are slightly larger than the standard racquets. Their selling point is that their sweet spots are about twice as large as regular racquets. Contrary to popular belief, oversized racquets do move well in the air. It's just a matter of getting used to them.

No man has done more to revolutionize the game than Howard Head, the inventor of the Prince racquet. Since its beginning it has been one of the most popular racquets on the market. Now, almost all racquet manufacturers have developed oversized racquets. These oversized racquets vary, but their sweet spots are about three-and-a-half times that of a regular racquet. Some racquet experts claim that their oversized racquets dampen vibration better than conventional racquets. Another advantage of the larger racquets is they enable you to get the balls you normally wouldn't. This results in added confidence. The only disadvantage I can see from their use is that players may have a tendency to get lazy, knowing they don't have to move as much.

The first important aspect in choosing a racquet is the proper grip. If you use a racquet with the wrong size grip, it can cause wrist and arm problems, not to mention shoulder and elbow problems as well. Grips vary in size from 4 to 5 inches with one-eighth inch increments. The theory used to be that the larger the grip size the more control you would have. In the past twenty years the theory has been revised to using the proper grip according to your hand size. To find your proper grip size you can:

1. Measure from your life line to the tip of your ring finger.
2. When you hold the racquet you should be able to place a finger between your fingers and the fatty part of your hand, the area below the thumb. It should fit in there comfortably, with neither too much of a gap, nor too snuggly.
3. You can also get a good idea by trying out racquets with different grip sizes. You can usually rent or borrow a demonstration racquet at any local racquet club.

The weight of a racquet varies only by about 3 ounces, which seems like nothing, but you can really feel the difference. Racquets are categorized into three weight classes: light, medium, and heavy, with light racquets usually being preferred. Medium and heavy racquets are specially weighted for larger tennis players. This added weight gives them a better feeling, and more control. If you are using a racquet too light for you, or too heavy, you will know it. The racquet will either feel like a toothpick or a war club in your hand.

The balance in a racquet also varies a little from even balance throughout the racquet to handle, light or heavy. The racquet head may be light or heavy. The lighter and more evenly balanced racquets are usually preferred. Heavier balanced racquets are used by larger tennis players for obvious reasons.

Racquets also vary in flexibility from flexible to stiff. Flexibility is found primarily in the head of the racquet. Racquets are constructed from a variety materials, with new materials being tried and tested every day. Each racquet has its own characteristics and advantages. This makes choosing a racquet even more difficult.

Racquet construction materials range from:

1. Wood.
2. Metal.
3. Fiberglass.
4. Composite.
5. Graphite.
6. And who knows what the future might bring?

Wood racquets are usually made from ash and hickory, with many other wood varieties used for cosmetic purposes. Some playing pros say you get a better feel for the ball using wood and so get better control. The average price for a wood racquet is $30 to $50. Wood racquets start to lose some of their "zip" within a year. On the average they are usable up to five years.

Metal racquets are constructed of aluminum and steel. They are constructed with an open throat for less wind resistance and added power. Recently some wood racquets have this same characteristic. A good player is said to get 10 percent more power using a metal racquet, though that is relative. Some metal racquets have a trampoline effect that catapults the ball. Though this effect will give you more power, it also takes away some of your control, and the racquet has a tendency to vibrate more. Due to their ease of maneuverability some players' stroke mechanics can suffer. This suffering stems from not having to work so hard to hit the ball. The price for a metal racquet is about the same as for a wood racquet.

Fiberglass racquets are made from one or two layers of fiberglass.

These are fairly strong racquets and can give you added power. The price range for fiberglass racquets is about the same as it is for wood or metal.

A relatively new style of racquet on the market today is the composite racquet. These racquets are constructed of two or more materials such as wood and fiberglass to form a racquet with the best qualities of each substance. The price of these racquets starts at nearly sixty dollars.

Graphite racquets are the newest type of racquet sold today. These racquets have the fine qualities of being light and strong at the same time. You get plenty of power while losing very little control. Some players say that some graphite racquets are too stiff, and that this stiffness can cause arm problems. These are nice racquets if you can afford them. They start at around a hundred dollars.

All racquets claim to give you more control, but I find that impossible. Control is relative, *you* control the ball, not the racquet.

When buying a racquet I would recommend staying away from racquets that are already prestrung, unless they are a name brand. Though the price may be less, the general quality, including the strings, is usually of poor quality.

Before you buy any racquet check the labeling. You will find some racquets have been mislabeled. Also check for any flaws in the racquet. You want to be sure you get what you are paying for.

In caring for your racquet please:

1. Don't throw it.
2. Scrape it on the court as little as possible.
3. Don't expose it to extreme temperatures.

If you take good care of your racquet, it will take care of you.

Balls

TENNIS BALLS ARE THE MOST underrated piece of tennis equipment. They are important because they can effect your game and fun. They have changed considerably since the game's emergence. The original balls were made of strips of cloth stitched together with thread. Later they were made of leather stuffed with wool, feathers, and other materials. I bet they didn't bounce too well. These first balls and ones made later had no specifications. Now all balls must pass rigid rules passed by the ILTA and approved by the USLTA. If approval is not stated on the can of balls, they might be of improper size, or off weight, which will cause inaccurate flight and bounce. Approximately 90,000,000 tennis balls are sold annually throughout the world.

There are four main colors of balls sold: yellow, white, and orange, and two-tone, yellow and orange. Eighty to ninety percent of all balls sold annually in the United States are yellow in color. The reason for yellow's popularity is that tests have proven they are easier to see. This color is used in most tournaments. Wimbledon is one of the few exceptions. White balls are used in this major tournament, because white balls are more easily seen on grass. Orange balls are the least used balls, even though they are said to show up better at night.

The newest type of ball to come on the market is the two-tone ball. The two different colors are supposed to make them stand out more and make them easier to watch.

Through more rigid tests, manufacturers have developed a heavy-duty tennis ball. This ball consists of new synthetic fibers that make them last longer on hard courts.

There are also pressureless balls on the market that contain a thicker core. Usually four balls are packed in each box. Pressureless balls last longer when stored and tend to play longer.

The disadvantages of these balls are that they:

1. Sound different.
2. Fly slower in the air.
3. Tend to bounce lower.
4. Are a little heavier.

With the disadvantages out numbering the advantages, most players prefer the pressure balls.

When you purchase your balls, remember to check them, if possible, before you leave. If you do buy a can containing one or more balls that are low on pressure—this does happen occasionally—then return it. The store or club should exchange it for you.

The price of tennis balls, unfortunately, has gone up like everything else. A can of balls usually ranges from $2 to $4. Watch for sales; you can save yourself some money. Through tennis ball manufacturers, it is possible to buy "seconds," balls cosmetically imperfect. In most cases you usually have to buy a gross of them. When you do you can get a good discount.

Fortunately for tennis ball manufacturers, but not for you, balls are not made to last forever. Keep this in mind once you open the can. Their shelf life is not very long, so use them as often as possible. No revolutionary ideas have been found to make them last longer. One device on the market now is a pressure pump. While your balls are in the pressure pump can, pressure is pumped in to keep the balls more alive. Some players have even resorted to putting tennis balls in the refrigerator hoping to keep them active longer. Maybe you can think of a solution and make a fortune.

Strings

TENNIS STRINGS TODAY FALL INTO three main categories: nylon, gut, and the more popular synthetic or manmade gut. Monofilament nylon strings, made of one strand of nylon, have been replaced by a better quality multifilament nylon string, made from a number of strands bonded together.

These nylon strings come in a variety of types. The three main kinds are: oil filled, wire impregnated, and woven. Oil filled has its core filled with oil; wire impregnated has steel wire embedded in it. This nylon, due to the wire, is of a stronger quality and lasts longer. Woven strings, after some use, fray in the same way gut does, and I feel, play the best of the nylon category. Nylon strings vary in price, depending on the store or club, from $8 to $15. All so-called beginners should use a type of nylon string. Most players can't feel any difference between nylon and gut string, so why pay the difference? Nylon strings have four advantages over gut:

1. Cost less.
2. String up easier and faster.
3. Can be used in all types of weather.
4. Last longer.

Gut strings on the other hand, if you can afford them, are preferred by most advanced players. Gut strings, contrary to popular belief, are not made from cats. This will be a relief to you cat lovers. They are made of thin strips of intestines from lambs and hogs wound tightly together. Gut strings come in different gauges or thicknesses. The thinner the gauge has more resilience but less durability.

214

The advantages to gut are:

1. More resilience.
2. Holds the ball longer on the strings.
3. Can give you a little more power, depending upon your ability.
4. Better control, also depending on your ability.

The disadvantages include:

1. Higher costs—$20 to $50 due to finer quality and care in stringing.
2. Shouldn't be used under poor weather conditions.
3. Won't last as long.

Synthetic string is becoming more and more popular since it takes the advantages of both nylon and gut and combines them to form the so-called "perfect" string. Synthetic string plays similar to gut, but at nearly half the cost.

The tension of your strings is your personal preference. Though it is relative, it is said that the lower the tension the more control you have, and the greater the tension the more power you have. Some authorities feel that the opposite is true. If you have any questions on the right tension for you, check with your local pro or follow the racquet manufacturer's suggestions. As a general rule of thumb beginners' racquets should be strung from fifty to fifty-five pounds, and more advanced players from fifty-five to sixty-two pounds. The pounds refer to the pounds of pressure on the strings per square inch. A frequently asked question is how often should I get my racquet restrung? The answer varies due to your own personal preference. It will also depend on the type of strings you use, how often you play, your ability, and how well you take care of your strings.

When you do get your racquet restrung, check the string job first before you accept it. You should be thoroughly satisfied with it before paying for it. When you receive your racquet the strings should show no wear, no strings should be crossed on the outside of the frame, and all the strings should be tight, including the last one. If any of these flaws occur, politely ask to have your racquet restrung at no cost.

Your strings can make a difference, so take care of them. In caring for your strings: hit only tennis balls, don't play in rainy weather, and try to avoid scraping your racquet on the court.

Grips

AS YOU KNOW, YOUR RACQUET SHOULD FEEL comfortable in your hand, and this is where your grip becomes important. The better your racquet feels the more confidence you will have, consequently the better you will play.

There are three main types of grips:

1. Flat and smooth.
2. Perforated.
3. Raised.

All three have a different feel, and each has its own advantages. It is up to you to pick the best one for you.

The flat and smooth grip is the most popular due to its comfortable feel. Most racquets are sold with this type of grip. The other two types are not as well known.

Perforated grips are grips containing holes throughout the grip. This promotes air circulation and is supposed to cause less perspiration on the hand.

The raised grip has raised strips of leather throughout the grip. This enables some players to get a firmer grip on the racquet.

There are two main brands of grips: calfskin and cowhide. Calfskin is better quality; cowhide is less expensive. Manufacturers have now developed a synthetic grip which they claim absorbs moisture more readily. Also on the market is gauze tape that wraps directly over the grip to absorb moisture.

You will find that the better quality racquets are sold with better quality grips. Two-handed backhand players should be aware that grip manufacturers make a grip specially designed for you. It is long enough for both your hands. You will find them flat and smooth and of fine quality.

The price for a grip, including wrapping it, varies from $5 to $10. You can save some money by buying your own grips through various companies and wrapping it yourself. In no time you will find that changing your grip is easy and fun. It will give you a sense of pride and accomplishment, besides saving you some money. The tools needed for doing this include: tacks or staples, hammer, glue, tape, and razor blade or scissors.

When removing the old grip check to see how it is fastened, usually with either a tack or a staple. Once the old grip is completely off, clean off any debris left by the used grip. Now you are ready to apply the new grip. Make sure the butt cap is securely fastened before attaching the new grip. It may need an additional staple. Tack or staple the tapered end of the grip to the butt. Next begin wrapping the new grip around the handle in a clockwise direction, making sure to have a slight overlap. The initial turn should just cover the tack or staple. As you continue to wrap pull tight, barely overlapping the edge of the preceding wrap, making sure there are no gaps in between the wraps. When you reach the end of the grip, tack or staple it in place. Cut off any excess grip so there won't be an uneven finish. For the finishing touch, wrap some trim tape around the top of the grip to give it a neat appearance.

You know it is time for a new grip when your old one begins: cracking, discoloring, and coming apart.

Proper caring for your grip will increase its life and make it feel better. Clean your grip when you feel it needs it or after every other time you play. You can clean your grip with soap and water, rubbing alcohol—though it might tend to dry out the grip, or a spray cleaner that is on the market.

Setting up Your Own Tennis Program

WHEN SETTING UP A TENNIS PROGRAM, or any type of program for that matter, you have a big responsibility before you. It is your job as organizer to provide the best possible program for the participants that you possibly can.

As you set up your program it is important to establish some attainable long-range goals. Your goals will vary slightly depending upon your particular situation. Some of your goals might be:

1. To promote the sport of tennis.
2. To promote physical fitness.

217

3. To introduce the participants to another carry-over sport.
4. To keep the "kids" off the streets.
5. To introduce another type of profession.

After your goals have been set, start setting up your program. In order to have a successful program you must first have six key ingredients:

1. Organization—this is one of the keys to anything you do. A good program takes plenty of organization. To have a program run smoothly, every detail needs to be thought through and planned. You cannot set up a program overnight.

Organization is a must if the participants are to have a worthwhile and enjoyable experience.

2. Motivation—when organizing any program, motivation is one of the keys. It will be important to get and keep your students excited about the program. Here are some ways to motivate your students:

Show films—instructional as well as various tournaments.
Have a guest speaker come in to talk about the sport, and to do some demonstrating.
Give a singles and doubles exhibition.
Have a bulletin board showing the students' favorite professionals.

3. Facility—your facility does not necessarily have to be a tennis complex or even a court. Almost any area about the size of a court will do: a gymnasium, a cafeteria, or a playground. Masking tape will work for your lines, though it won't last a long time.
4. Equipment—good quality and reasonably priced equipment is not as hard to come by as one might think. All you need to do is ask around a lot and compare. I bet if you "play your cards right" a local racquet club or college would be willing to give you a helping hand. If money is no problem, buy good quality equipment that will last longer, enabling you to get your money's worth. Unfortunately in most cases, money is the determining factor, so this will not apply.

If I were setting up a program, I would first go to a local racquet club. In most cases they are willing to donate old balls, unclaimed racquets, old rebound nets and old nets. Whatever contribution the club makes would more than pay for itself in the long run. Once someone gets the "tennis bug" he usually starts looking for his own club or at least professional instruction.

The basic equipment you will need, are racquets, balls, a net, and ball containers.

> Racquets—not necessarily one per person if the class has all the same size students. They can share, because a couple of the students will be picking up the balls at all times. If you have to buy your own racquets they will cost you $15 and up.
> Balls—the number will depend on the size of your class. I would say approximately twenty-five balls for each student should be sufficient. If you have to buy new balls, they will cost from $2.00 a can on up. Look for discounts.
> Net—the net does not have to be a tennis net, though it helps. I have used a volley ball net and that will work. As a last resort you can very easily make your net posts. This will involve filling two old tires with concrete and placing a steel pipe in each tire before the concrete sets. When the concrete has hardened you can stretch any type of net between them and you are set to go. If you want a good net you should expect to pay $80 and up. You can also purchase the net and post together forming a portable net. This will cost from $300 to $600.
> Ball container—you need at least one container to hold all the balls. A laundry basket or wastebasket can work, but if you can *honestly* get a shopping cart that would be the best.

Other pieces of equipment that would be nice to have are: a rebound net, divider nets, ball machine, ball hoppers, and a wall.

Rebound nets—are not necessary, but they sure can help. You can serve over them or one to two players can rally into them. A new one will cost you at least $100.

Net dividers—are the woven mesh nets that are used to separate courts. Again these are not necessary, but they make it safer if you have more than one court. These will cost you anywhere from 13 cents to 20 cents per square foot.

Ball machine—is another luxury item. They are great for repetition work but will not take the place of an instructor. These machines usually start at around $275.

Ball hoppers—are devices especially made to pick up tennis balls. These will save the back muscles. They cost around $25.

Wall—if you have a wall that you can use as a rally wall, so much the better. Place a line of tape representing the height of a net on the wall. Depending on the size of the wall, two or more players should be able to safely rally against the wall.

5. Qualified instruction—you will usually find this key ingredient the hardest one to get. In most cases your instructors will be non-professionals, though highly motivated. Your budget usually cannot afford to have a local professional come in to instruct. It should be up to the administration department to get the best possible instructors. If at all possible, try to get certified instructors. They should be certified by either the USPTA or PTR.

Here is where I feel local professionals could do themselves a favor. They should offer a course on how to teach tennis. The course should be geared for teaching the basic techniques to avoid the development of bad habits and to encourage further instruction at the professional level. That way tennis would reach more people and the professionals would get more students. Everyone would benefit.

6. Willing students—due to popularity of the sport, this area should be the least of your worries. You would be well advised not to force anyone into the program. When this happens, so do your problems.

The most important segment of your program is the instruction that should consist of at least ten one hour lessons with the class meeting once a week. If you have really young beginners, you might want to consider giving them half-hour lessons. The goals for each lesson should be:

For the students to learn about tennis.
For the students to get some good exercise.
For the students to have fun.

If at all possible, each group should be chosen according to their ability. This way a less experienced player won't be pressured by a more advanced players. Also avoid classifying players by beginners, advanced beginners, and so forth. Instead let them choose their own group name, or maybe give them the name of a professional team such as the "Vikings." A beginner will still be a beginner, but at least he won't be stereotyped as such.

Try to keep the groups to a minimum of six players, otherwise there will be too much confusion and not enough time to give each student the individual attention he deserves.

Your ten week course could follow a pattern like this:

Week 1—introduce the grips, eye–hand coordination games, relay races, rules, and mini-tennis.
Week 2—Forehand.
Week 3—Backhand.
Week 4—Volley.
Week 5—Overhead.
Week 6—Serve.
Week 7—Return of serve.
Week 8—Approach shot.
For the first eight weeks the lessons should consist of one-half hour of instruction and the last one-half hour for movement drills relating to the particular stroke of the day.
Week 9—A mini version of a tournament.
Week 10—A skills test and an awards program. The skills test can consist of hitting balls to various spots on the court using the various strokes. A similar test can be used on the first day to group the students. This type of testing is one means of evaluating your program.

When the students have free time during the week encourage open play. You can even set up a challenge ladder for the more competitive players.

This program may be the first experience the person has with tennis so be sure to make it enjoyable and have fun with it.

Movement Drills and Games

MOVEMENT DRILLS ARE CAREFULLY planned drills that aid in improving your tennis game. Besides improving your game, these drills should be enjoyable and challenging. While drilling, the emphasis should be on control, footwork, and good form. The benefits from these movement drills and games are:

1. They enable you to hit a lot of balls in a minimum amount of time. This is one of the keys for improvement.
2. They give you a good idea of your stroking ability.
3. They are a fine motivating factor.
4. If there is a shortage of courts they allow a number of players to practice at the same time.
5. If you have a weakness, drills are one of the best means for improving it.
6. They are good exercise.

When you go out to practice with one or more players, it is important that you be well organized and that you use your time wisely. In order to do this you may want to chart what you want to work on and your goals for the practice session. Each drill requires at least ten to fifteen minutes in order to get the proper benefit from it. There are drills and games here for all ability levels. Be sure while drilling to use lively balls, otherwise you won't be getting true bounces and that will ruin your drills and games.

Start out slowly and increase pace when you are ready. Some drills will require the use of a "ball feeder," a player who tosses the balls to another player. His responsibility is critical to the outcome of a practice drill. It is his job to set the other players up with balls that are easy to hit, ones that are the proper height, pace, and distance for each particular player. In most cases the balls should be thrown underhand and from the same side of the net as the player hitting the balls. One caution: don't stand directly in front of the player hitting the ball. I wonder why? Also, for hitters, avoid directing your shots toward the feeder. That's a good way lose friends!

Here are some of the many varieties of movement drills. Feel free to make up your own.

222

Ghost doubles

Ghost doubles derives its name from having a so-called ghost as your partner. In this modified doubles game, doubles is played but with just two players. This is a very good game for developing control and practicing the shots you would use in a regular doubles game. It is also a fine game for players who don't like to cover the whole court or can't physically manage to do so.

The object of the game is to keep the ball in play using half the court either crosscourt or on one specific side, which you predetermine before play begins. While using the usual scoring system, whenever you hit the ball to the wrong section of the court you lose the point. I've even seen two games going on the same court at the same time.

Rally in the alley

As the name implies, the object of this drill is to control the ball in the alley. Work on both the forehand and backhand sides of the court. The purpose of this drill is to practice your ground strokes, while at the same time working on your control and down-the-line shots.

Close order volley drill

This drill can be done with two to four players, each at their homebase at the net. The primary purpose of this drill is to improve your reflex volleys. When more than two players are participating this is an excellent drill for working on control, by hitting the ball in a specific pattern.

Two on one drill

This drill can be done anywhere on the court when you have two players team up against one. The aim of this drill is to let everyone work on their strokes, while giving the player by himself a very good work-out. In this drill you can either play out a series of points or just rally. The strokes you need to work on will determine where the players start on the court.

223

Seven ball drill

This all-court drill requires one player to start at his homebase behind the baseline, while a ball feeder positions himself at his homebase at the net. The player at the baseline starts out by hitting a wide forehand and then returns to his homebase. Then he moves over and hits a wide backhand, again returning to his homebase. Next the feeder places a ball to be hit as an approach shot. After the approach shot has been executed, the player moves up to his homebase at the net. From there he will hit alternating volleys, ending up with an overhead. Emphasis in this drill is placed on moving to the ball with the racquet in position.

Two ball drill

This is the top drill for advanced players. Two to four players can participate. The ultimate goal is to keep two balls in play at the same time. Start out with just one ball until you get your timing down, then have someone put another ball in play. Once you have mastered keeping two balls in play, more balls can be added.

Rally crosscourt and down-the-line

These drills involve keeping the ball in play by rallying either crosscourt or down-the-line. Besides working on control, work on depth. Set realistic goals you can obtain each time you use this drill. For a variation of this drill, have one player hit all his balls crosscourt, while his partner hits down-the-line. You can see that this drill involves quite a bit of movement.

One up–one back

When choosing this drill you can use the whole court. For added difficulty, split the court in half. The player at the net puts the ball in play, with both players keeping the ball in play for a set number of strokes. Once that number has been reached, both players try to win the point. This drill is designed to work on consistency, as well as lobs and passing shots.

224

Rally quota

This drill can be used playing either mini-tennis or using the whole court. In either case the object is to keep the ball in play as long as possible. In using this drill you are working on control and patience.

Dead-Ball

This game is specially designed for youngsters just learning the game. Almost any number of players can take part, as long as it doesn't get too congested. This is a team game. The object is to prevent the ball from rolling on your side of the net. The ball can be hit as many times as it takes to get it over the net. Once the ball rolls, yell "dead-ball," and start the next point.

Volley touch the baseline drill

From the name of this drill you can guess why it is recommended for advanced players in top physical condition. The drill involves executing a good volley, then immediately running back and touching the baseline, and then moving up to the net again. Before you start, set the number of good volleys a player has to hit before he can rest. This drill is a good conditioner. It is also good for working on your volleys and split-steps.

Serve and volley

In this drill you practice the serve and volley tactic that you use in both singles and doubles. For best results have the ball feeder positioned near the service line with a hand full of balls. After the player serves and immediately approaches the net, the feeder sets the server up for his first volley, then second volley, and finally an overhead. Your first priority is to get the serve in and then think about the next stroke. To make the drill more challenging, make the server get the serve in before he can even attempt his first volley.

Return serve and rush

Like the serve and volley drill, this aggressive tactic is used in both singles and doubles. This time the feeder is also the server. He should position himself near the service line instead of the baseline to insure a high percentage of serves in. The returner's first and main objective is to get the ball back into play. To make this drill more realistic, make the returner hit a good return before he can continue to the net. After a good return is made, he proceeds to the net position for a series of volleys and finishes with an overhead. Again, emphasis is on concentrating on one stroke at a time, and your famous split-step.

Three balls across

This drill starts with one or more players at one side of the baseline and a ball feeder at his usual position near the other service line. The feeder places or hits a series of three balls to three spots along the baseline. The spots will vary according to the players' ability. Do not move for any ball until it is hit, otherwise you will be just running through your shots. Forehands as well as backhands can be practiced with this drill. Emphasis is placed on getting your racquet back early and moving with the racquet in position.

Three balls forward

This drill begins with one or more players behind their homebase at the baseline. The ball feeder stands near the other service line. The player at the baseline first hits either a forehand or backhand, then hits an approach shot, then finishes with a volley. The purpose of this drill is to work on your forward movement.

Back court game

Two to four players start out at their homebases behind the baseline. After any player puts a ball into play you rally out the point, keeping the ball deep in the court. If the ball is hit in the service courts, the point is lost. The object of this game is to work on depth, keeping the ball deep in the court so your opponent can't take advantage of a short ball.

Australian or Canadian doubles

Australian doubles sometimes referred to as Canadian doubles, is a game played with just three players. This is a great game for working on all your strokes and strategies, as well as a fine conditioning game for the player by himself.

The same rules apply to this version of doubles, except for the area of the court the doubles team can hit into. The player by himself can use the whole court, while the doubles team can only hit into the singles court. However, for the hardiest of players, or for players who need to work on their court coverage, the player by himself can try to cover the whole court.

The Most Asked Questions about Tennis

1. What causes my grip to slip?
Answer: Contrary to what most players think, it is not your grip size, though in some cases, it might very well be. Usually the problem is your eyes. You are not watching or concentrating on the ball well enough, consequently you hit an off-center shot. No matter how tight you squeeze your grip, an off-center shot or mis-hit will cause your racquet to turn.

2. When do I need new shoes?
Answer: The amount of time between new shoes will vary with every player. Some players are harder on their shoes than others. When a section of the shoe starts to wear thin, that is the time to start looking for a new pair. In most cases the soles wear out first, though if you drag your toes, especially when you serve, your toe area may wear out first. If you don't repair your shoes by one of several ways now on the market, or get a new pair, you are running the risk of serious injury. A faulty pair of shoes can cause you to slip, turn an ankle, or worse.

227

3. Do I need a larger racquet?

Answer: Only you can really answer this question. Your racquet is a very personal part of your game and should not be taken lightly. More and more players every day are turning to the oversized racquets for good reasons. These larger racquets give you more confidence, enable you to reach farther, and have a larger sweet spot. These are good reasons to switch, however don't change because you think they will correct your faulty strokes—they won't. Only lessons and hard work on the practice court will do that. Before you spend quite a bit of money purchasing a racquet, try out a demonstrator model at your local club or a friend's to make sure this is what you want. Large racquets are not for everyone, so be sure before you make the change.

4. Which shoes are best?

Answer: Again it is personal preference, and everyone is different. No one brand of shoe is best for everyone. Shoes differ as much as racquets do. Some have higher arches, while others have more cushion. You are after the pair that is the most comfortable for your feet. Be sure to get ones that have plenty of cushion so your feet will withstand the punishment of a long match.

5. What causes my racquet to vibrate?

Answer: If your racquet isn't cracked or if you have a metal racquet and a little piece of plastic hasn't come loose, then your eyes did it to you again. You are hitting too many balls near the edge of your racquet. This can eventually cause hand and arm problems, so take heed and concentrate on the ball more.

6. How early should I start my child playing tennis?

Answer: First you must ask yourself why you want your child to learn to play the game. Is it because you want him to be rich and famous so that he can support you? Or is it because you want him to have fun, get some good exercise, develop sportsmanship, meet more peers, and learn about himself? Very few players ever make it to the top echelon of the pro circuit because of the special physical and mental talents it takes, so choosing the first reason to start your son or daughter is unrealistic in most cases.

The answer to this question will vary with each child. Your key is to start them when *they* start to show an interest. If you try to start them before they are ready, it will be a frustrating experience for everyone and they may lose interest forever. Remember their first experience should be fun. For this reason there is no set age when to start a child.

David, age four, enjoys being on the court. In fact, we get into trouble if we don't take him with us. He has learned to hit a forehand and a backhand and is experimenting with a serve.

Matthew, at age one-and-a-half, likes to tag along. He tries to play tennis like his big brother. It is time to get him his own racquet, because David complains that Matthew is dragging his racquet too much.

You as parents can influence them. Children from the earliest stages of development try to imitate their parents. So it is important for you as parents to set a good example for them on and off the court. If you play tennis yourself, take them to the court with you so they can be with you, as well as experience the game. I started playing at the age of eleven, however, our first son started experiencing the game before he could walk by being on the court with us, and playing with our tennis balls. Our second son started the same way.

Here are a few ways to develop eye–hand coordination that every child will need, no matter what they do: playing with a balloon, throwing balls, hitting balls rolled to them, and using a paddle with a little ball attached by a rubber band.

Their first racquet should *not* be one of yours, which frequently is the case. Even if it has been cut off, the weight will still be wrong. Start them off with their own junior racquet especially made for their size.

Group lessons can be started whenever you think they are ready. Lessons should only be for half an hour at first due to their short attention span.

7. How do I know if a teaching pro is a good one?
Answer: A good way is to ask your friends and see if they have had any lessons with the teaching pro, and what they think. Here are some criteria for rating a teaching pro:

    a. A member of USPTA.
    b. A member of the PTR.
    c. Has a neat appearance.
    d. Is in good physical condition.
    e. Has a better than average playing ability.
    f. Shows a willingness to improve.
    g. Does things for no reward, freebies.
    h. Has more than a basic knowledge of the game.
    i. Shows good sportsmanship.
    j. Is good in personal relations.
    k. Has a good personality.
    l. Is prompt.
    m. Willing to work weekends and odd hours but not all the time.
    n. Sets an atmosphere conducive to learning.
    o. Shows a genuine interest in the students.
    p. Is well organized.
    q. Has a well stocked pro shop.

r. Remembers your name.

s. Uses teaching aids.

t. Isn't on an ego trip.

u. You learn something new during your lesson.

v. Communicates well and enough during your lesson.

w. Doesn't spend more time talking than letting you hit.

x. Uses player analysis cards. These cards chart your progress and state your strong and weak points.

y. Group lessons should consist of no more than a 6 to 1 ratio. Even then a ball machine must be used, so no one is standing around, and so they can hit plenty of balls.

z. In a group lesson the pro should not be helping one student while all the others are just watching.

8. Should I join a club and if so, which one?

Answer: The choice is yours. It will depend on a number of variables:

a. How serious you are.

b. How often you play.

c. If you can afford it.

d. If you really enjoy playing.

e. If you enjoy the social aspects the club can offer.

Depending on your size of town you may or may not have a choice. The club may be the only one around, or you may have many to choose from. If that is the case here are some suggestions to keep in mind when choosing a club:

a. Does it have qualified teaching pros?

b. Is there quality personnel throughout the club?

c. Ask your friends about the club to get their opinion.

d. Is it well organized?

e. Are their programs for everyone?

f. Do they have enough courts?

g. Is there a weight room and strength training programs?

h. Do they have a sauna?

i. Is it well kept?

j. Are the pro shop attendants friendly?

k. Is the membership increasing?

l. Do they make you feel welcome?

m. Do they hold exhibitions and tournaments?

n. Membership price.

o. Do they provide a baby-sitting service?

Once you have compared the various clubs, choose the one best suited for your needs as a player.

9. Which tennis resort should I go to?
Answer: With the number of tennis resorts all over the country, you really have a tough choice to make. You will find all resorts have their good qualities, and if you enjoy being pampered, the resort life is for you. Most resorts cater to all types of players, and one caters just to the tournament players. With prices what they are today, you want to be sure to get the most for your money. Before you choose one you should to find out as much as you can about it. Things you would like to know should include:

a. How much free court time?
b. Learn about all the programs.
c. Free time activities available.
d. Are there any programs for the children?

How do you find out about the tennis resorts available? Ask both your club pro and your friends. They should be able to recommend some. The two national tennis magazines on the market are loaded with information about resorts all over the world. You could also ask a travel agent.

I can personally recommend the one I worked for. It is a first class organization, run by highly trained personnel, and well worth a visit. It is John Gardiner's Tennis Ranch in Scotsdale, Arizona.

When you go to the resort of your choice, be sure to be in good shape before you go. Otherwise you will get too tired and sore to have fun.

10. Is tennis a good exercise for losing weight?
Answer: I would like to be able to say it is a great exercise for losing weight, however, it is not as good as some other sports. It can help with weight reduction, along with proper diet.

11. Will a couple of lessons improve my game?
Answer: Yes and no. Yes, if you practice what you have been taught between lessons and no, if you don't. Just like anything else, practice has to help. When you are taking a lesson, you must keep an open mind and be willing to make a few minor changes. In a couple of lessons you should only cover two to four aspects of the game. Most

players want to cover the entire game in one lesson, and that is simply impossible. If you keep this in mind, a couple of lessons should improve your game, but it won't make you a superstar overnight.

12. How do the pros on television make it look so easy?
Answer: In one word—concentration! If you would ask one of the top pros what they think about on the court, they would answer, "The ball." All their thoughts are directed toward the ball. Even with their total concentration, it isn't as easy for them as it looks. Remember, it has taken them countless hours on the court to bring their level of play up to where it is. Through these hours of hard work they have developed their skills to become second nature. They are as much at home on the tennis court as we are in our living rooms.

Unfortunately for us our skills are not as refined as theirs, so we just can't concentrate on the ball as we should. We have too many other things running through our minds like get the racquet back, change grips, watch the ball, get to the ball, where will I hit it, and I hope they miss my shot. Besides tennis we are thinking about the things we usually find ourselves cluttering our minds with like, "what will I fix for dinner, or should I be at the office working on my big business deal?"

When you're on the court try thinking of just one thing at a time and shut everything else out. Our minds just can't handle thinking of more than one thing at a time.

13. Am I too old to play tennis?
Answer: Probably not, unless you're physically unable to move. However, since tennis can be a strenuous sport, use good judgment, and if you have any doubts, consult with your physician first. If he gives you the go-ahead signal, start out slowly and take adequate rest periods so that you don't get too tired.

14. I am a "B" player. Is it advisable to teach my wife or child how to play?
Answer: It will depend on your patience and your knowledge of the game. When you teach a spouse or offspring it is too easy to expect too much. This can cause ill feelings. Your knowledge should include the teaching aspects of the game, because you don't want bad habits to develop. In most cases it is much easier and smoother for your family relations if you set up professional group lessons for either your wife or your child. This can be done at very reasonable prices.

Don't take me wrong, I am not saying do not go out on the court and have fun with your family. On the contrary, tennis can be a very good family sport, and is more enjoyable if shared by the whole family. Just don't expect your spouse or child to be the next club champion, and when the teaching aspects are too demanding for you to handle, send them to a professional.

15. How often do you have to play or practice in order to improve?
Answer: That depends a lot on your ability now, and your definition of "improve." If you just play once a week you are lucky to stay at the level you're at. With most players it takes playing at least two to three times a week in order to improve their ability level. This is harder for many of you working men and women than it is for junior players. So keep that in mind when you desire more rapid improvement.

16. When receiving serve do I have to stand within the lines surrounding the court?
Answer: No, you can stand anywhere on your side of the court.

17. Can I serve in singles from behind the baseline in the alley portion of the court?
Answer: No.

18. Can I volley a return of serve?
Answer: No, you must let it bounce first.

19. How can I become a tennis pro?
Answer: First, which type of professional do you mean . . . teaching or playing (touring pro)? If your ambition is to be a touring pro, then you are not alone. Thousands of aspiring juniors, as well as young and not so young adults, set their sights on playing professionally in the finals on center court at Wimbledon, before thousands of spectators with either Jimmy Connors or Chris Evert Lloyd on the other side of the net. Unfortunately for most players, this goal is a little unrealistic. Since there is so much competition, you have to be more than a head above the others mentally and physically.

Rankings is the name of the game and your scale for judging your ability and potential. Very few players have ever made it to the top level without first being ranked somewhere previously.

The following is the ranking list to judge your progress. If you are ranked at one level, then your next goal is to be ranked in the next level above. The scale is as follows:

1. World
2. National
3. Sectional
4. State
5. City
6. Club

In order to be considered for ranking, you first need to be a member of the United States Tennis Association, USTA, and play a minimum number of USTA sanctioned tournaments during the year.

Once you have reached either a state or preferably, a sectional ranking, you might like to try your hand at qualifying for professional tournaments in one of the "satellite" tournaments.

These tournaments are just one step below the major tours, with many fine quality players. In the draws you will find top juniors and tour veterans, trying to regain their form. The prize money is far below the scale of a major tournament, but at least there's not as much traveling. The tournament schedule is usually set up in specific regions of the country such as the south or midwest. Each tour consists of several tournaments lasting over the course of a few months. To find out the dates and location of such tournaments, contact the USTA.

If you think this might be the life for you and you qualify, remember it takes more than just walking on center court, playing an hour, and collecting your money. Most all the top pros have been playing all their lives at least eight hours every day. It takes a lot of hard work. Even then, there are no guarantees of making it.

You also must be willing to travel up to ten months a year. This sounds like fun and is for a while, but after the excitement wears off, you realize what the tour is all about. It's a lot of hard work, eating out all the time, and not sleeping in your own bed, not to mention the strain it puts on a relationship, unless the "other-half" is free to travel as well.

Becoming a teaching professional is not as easy or glamorous as most people think. First of all, remember you are becoming a *professional*. You must be willing to conduct yourself accordingly. The qualities needed for becoming a teaching professional were already stated in a previous question. Remember it takes much more than being able to play well.

If you are considering this profession, or for that matter any profession, I recommend that you start out at the bottom and work your way up. There are many summer teaching jobs available if you know where to look. First check the local club(s) and city programs.

They usually hire more help during the summer months. There are also numerous types of camps and resorts located throughout the country needing counselors and teaching help.

When you begin your career as an "apprentice" teaching pro, listen and learn from the more experienced teachers. It would be a good idea to take notes on the good points and ideas you have learned. The pay for these types of summer employment may not be the best, but in most cases they furnish room and board and some spending money. The main rewards you get will be the experiences and personal contacts. The contacts might be able to help you later.

After several summers of these teaching experiences, you should have a fairly good idea if you want to pursue this career permanently. If you think you might, I would recommend becoming certified as soon as possible by either or both the USPTA—United States Professional Tennis Association—and/or the PIR—Professional Tennis Registry. To become certified you will be required to take a written, playing, and teaching test. When an employer is looking for a teaching pro, this certification is one of the first things he looks for.

There are many very fine tennis organizations located throughout the country that I would highly recommend you attend, either as a student or a teaching pro. They can instruct you in the finer points of teaching and give a solid foundation on which to build your own style. Such types of organizations are: John Gardiner's Tennis Ranch, Dennis Van Der Meer Tennis University, Vic Braden Tennis College, John Newcombe's tennis facilities, and Harry Hopman's International Tennis, just to mention a few. These facilities, as well as many others, will give you more and varied experiences. The more experiences and teaching positions you have on your resume, the better your chances of landing a head pro job of your own. This is what most pros seek. I would *not* recommend changing jobs too often. I would say, depending on the circumstances, not to change jobs more often than every two years. If you do it might look like you can't hold a job or don't want to be tied down in any one place for any length of time.

These head pro positions are not as easy to come by as one might think. It is harder than in the past, due to the number of teaching pros on the market. This is where your many experiences and contacts come into play. As with everything else, knowing the right person can make all the difference in the world.

Pay at the top teaching levels can be very lucrative, and the benefits are good, but it will usually take years of hard work to get there.

As with any job, there are sacrifices you will have to make. Being a teaching professional, depending on where you work, can be a hard life with long hours. You will usually work some evenings and weekends, at least on Saturdays. In other places it may mostly be just seasonal work, with long dry spells. This can make for boring times and be financially unrewarding.

If this is the life for you, work hard or as they "pay your dues," and good luck.

Questions for You to Think About

1. Is it legal to hit the ball around the net posts?
Answer: If you find yourself in this predicament and your ability will allow you to do it, it is perfectly legal to hit the ball around the net posts. In most cases you will even win the point if it lands in the court. When the ball passes by the net posts it can be any height, as long as it doesn't touch the court.

2. Is it possible to hit the ball under the net and win the point?
Answer: I have never seen it done, and you probably won't either, but it is legal if you can do it. You ask how often does this freak shot occur? Very, very seldom. And it is recorded even less, in most cases it happens too fast to see.

This unusual act can only occur in an official singles match when additional net posts are placed in both alleys to raise the net to the required height. When the net is raised there will be a slight opening of a few inches where, if the ball is hit just right, it can pass under the net. As the ball passes under the net, it cannot touch your court or the net before it lands in the other court, otherwise you will lose the point. This is not a shot you want to spend a lot of time practicing, but one you should be aware of.

3. When can you hit the ball into the net, and still win the point?
Answer: Unfortunately not as often as you would like. This situation has probably happened to you, but you just didn't realize it. Here is an example of how it happens. You are playing someone who puts an unworldly amount of backspin on the ball. The ball hits your side of the court near the net. Before you realize what is happening, the ball

bounces back to your opponent's side of the court. Before you count the point as lost, it is legal, and this is the only time when it is. If you can't hit the ball on your side of the net, you can reach over to your opponent's side of the net and hit the ball. As long as you don't touch the net in the process, you can hit the ball anywhere in the court that you want to, even in the net, and you can still win the point, believe it or not!

4. How many times can you swing at the ball?
Answer: You can swing at the ball as many times as it takes to make contact with the ball. You usually see this happen more in doubles when one partner misses a ball, and his partner, who is backing him up, returns the ball. Or you may have seen someone miss an overhead completely and then, with great effort, hit it on the next swing. Once, in a demonstration, I saw a teaching pro whiff an overhead twice and somehow still hit it before he lost the point. That is really the hard way to win a point!

5. Do you have to play with a tennis racquet:
Answer: No! You can play with anything you like. But you must stick to whatever you start out with; you can't change to a racquet.

In or Out?

WHICH BALL IS OUT? Sure that was an easy question. Now let's make it a little harder. Place several balls on and near the baseline and stand near the other baseline and see if you can tell which balls are out. Then move up to the net and try your luck. You'll find it harder than you think. Then remember that when you're playing, you are moving and the ball is moving at the same time you are trying to call the lines. Besides that you are under pressure. So how can some of you think

238

that you can possibly call balls in or out on your opponent's side of the net? It's even hard for your opponent to call them, though they're on his side, but let him call them.He has a better view. I think some pros should take this test, don't you?

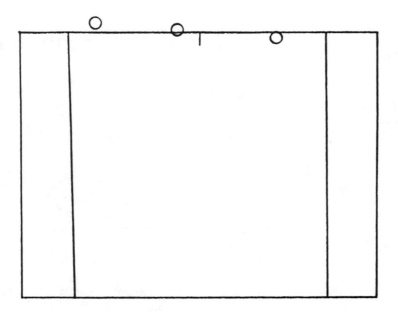

Additional Vocabulary

Ace or Service Ace—is any time a ball is served and is not touched by the receiver.

Amateur—any player not receiving financial rewards for playing.

Bye—in tournament play, when a player in a round doesn't have an opponent and automatically advances to the next round. This usually just happens in the first round.

Chip—is when you come under the ball. It can also be referred to as underspin.

Choke—is what happens to you in a pressure situation when you miss an easy shot. You get too nervous and tighten up.

Default—this happens when you are unable to finish a match due to any reason whatsoever, such as an injury. You automatically lose the match.

Dink—this is an off-pace shot, one which is hit without much pace. Many players have trouble playing "dinkers." A player hits these shots because he tries to do too much with them.

Double Hit—this occurs in doubles when both players hit the ball. You usually see this happen when the players are at the net.

Forced Error—this is when you lose the point due to your opponent's shot. It is one you hit that either went out or into the net.

Form—this is the style you use when you hit the ball.

Love Game—this is a service game you win when your opponent doesn't win a point.

Outright Winner—this is a shot, other than a serve, that your opponent can't get to to make the return.

Rallying—is the term used when you and your friends go out on the court and hit the ball back and forth. Too often I hear the word "volley" used in place of rally.

Service Break—is when you win a game that your opponent served.